This copy of

MOUNTAIN-PEAK
MYSTERY
by Carolyn Keene

belongs to

____

____

Other Sparrow Books
by Carolyn Keene

Mystery of the Stone Tiger
The Riddle of the Frozen Fountain
The Secret of the Silver Dolphin
Mystery of the Wax Queen
The Secret of the Minstrel's Guitar
The Phantom Surfer
The Secret of the Swiss Chalet
The Haunted Lagoon
Mystery of the Bamboo Bird
The Sierra Gold Mystery
The Secret of Lost Lake
The Winking Ruby Mystery
The Ghost in the Gallery
The Curious Coronation
The Hundred-Year Mystery

Carolyn Keene

MOUNTAIN-PEAK MYSTERY

SPARROW BOOKS

A Sparrow Book
Published by Arrow Books Limited
17-21 Conway Street, London W1P 6JD

An imprint of the Hutchinson Publishing Group

London Melbourne Sydney Auckland
Johannesburg and agencies
throughout the world

First Published in Great Britain by Severn House 1984
Sparrow edition 1984

Printed and bound in Great Britain by
Anchor Brendon Ltd, Tiptree, Essex

ISBN 0 09 932780 5

CONTENTS

CHAPTER I

The Roadblock

THE big brass knocker on the Danas' front door banged loudly. Louise and Jean, who were reading in the living room, looked up, startled.

"I wonder who it is?" Louise asked.

She rose from an overstuffed chair and went to admit the caller. A girl about fourteen years old stood outside. She was a pretty brunette, dressed in a light-blue trouser suit.

"Are you one of the Dana girls?" she asked.

"Yes. I'm Louise."

"My name is Tammi Hodge," the visitor replied. "My grandfather asked me to see you two about solving a mystery."

"Please come in," Louise said, smiling.

Jean had followed her sister to the door and now introduced herself. Intrigued by the thought of a mystery, the girls walked into the living room. Louise, a pretty, dark-haired seventeen-year-old, sat next to Tammi on the couch, while blonde Jean, who was a year younger, pulled up a chair.

"Now, tell us why your grandfather wanted you to see us," Louise began.

"I have a strange mystery to solve," Tammi replied. "Grandpa passed away a short time ago. My parents have been dead for many years, and I lived with Grandpa Hodge in his house on the mountain. I had been away at school, but I was called home because Grandpa was ill."

Tammi choked up at this point, and it took several seconds before she could go on. "One day, when I was alone with him, he began to gasp, and I knew he was going to die. I wanted to call the doctor, but he said no. He had something to tell me."

Again Tammi stopped speaking. The girl was so upset that she kept crossing and uncrossing her ankles and tapping on the arms of her chair.

Louise and Jean felt sorry for her and asked if she would like a cold drink.

"No, thank you," Tammi replied. "I want to finish my story. Grandpa grabbed my hand and said, 'I'm going to die. Listen carefully. I wrote a manuscript telling of a great discovery I made. It was stolen. Get the Dana girls to help you find—duplicate—mountain peak——' I begged him to let me go for help, but he wouldn't. Then he died."

Both Louise and Jean felt their eyes becoming

moist, and Louise put an arm around the girl's shoulders. "Would you like to wait a while before telling us the rest?" she asked.

Tammi shook her head. "No, I want to talk everything over with you now. I have no relatives. There were just Grandpa and me. In his will he left a request that the executor appoint a guardian for me."

"Who is the executor?" Jean asked.

"The Oak Falls Bank," Tammi replied. "They received a letter from a Miss Mathilde Price, written to her by Grandpa Hodge. In it he requested that she live with me until I come of age."

"Who's Miss Mathilde Price?" Jean asked.

"Oh, she's an old friend of Grandpa's. But she's a terrible person. I can't stand her!"

"Why?"

"Just imagine, the first thing she did when she arrived was to change everything around in the house. She went through each room and took it apart. We had a real battle when she started on my bedroom. I wouldn't let her touch anything."

"I can't blame you," Louise said sympathetically.

Tammi smiled. "Miss Mathilde became very angry. She told me she was in charge now and would arrange things the way she wanted to."

"Did she?"

"Well, she left my room alone for a while

and went to the next one. I can't explain how strange it all is—almost as if she were looking for something!"

Jean knitted her brows thoughtfully. "It seems odd, especially so soon after your grandfather's death."

Louise changed the subject. "Does Miss Mathilde know you came to see us?"

"Oh, no. I just ran out and took the bus." Tammi's eyes clouded up again. "I don't trust Miss Mathilde," she said, "and I know she doesn't care for me!"

"Why do you say that?" Jean asked. "Besides ripping the house apart, doesn't she treat you well?"

"She tries to be friendly sometimes," Tammi replied, "but I can tell it's false. She's very stern, and frankly I think she hates me!"

"I wonder why your grandfather asked her to be your guardian," Louise said.

"She was madly in love with him when they were both young," Tammi said. "He never mentioned it to me, but I heard about it from other people. I guess he wasn't interested, but they remained friends all their lives. He probably felt she would be glad to take care of me, but I think she's still mad because he didn't marry her and is now taking out her spite on me."

Louise nodded, then said, "Tammi, have you

any idea what your grandfather's last words meant?"

"None. But evidently he felt you could unlock his secret. Oh, please help me!"

The Danas were eager to take the case, but wondered if Miss Mathilde would permit them to visit the mountain-peak house.

"I won't let her keep you away!" Tammi said firmly.

At this moment Aunt Harriet walked into the room, and the girls introduced her to Tammi. Louise and Jean lived with their aunt and her brother Ned. He was captain of an ocean-going ship named the *Balaska*, and was now away on a trip.

"Tammi Hodge has a very interesting story," Louise told Miss Dana. "She lives up on the mountain peak. A Miss Mathilde Price is taking care of her, but Tammi doesn't care for the woman."

Aunt Harriet said sympathetically, "Oftentimes we don't like people at first, but later we get to love them."

Tammi's eyes flashed. "I'll never get to like that prim, scolding ex-schoolteacher. I feel sorry for the people who were her pupils. She's just awful, Miss Dana."

Tammi's story was related to Aunt Harriet, and she expressed her condolences to Tammi on the loss of her grandfather.

"Thank you," Tammi said. Then she turned to the girls. "How soon can you work on the mystery?"

Louise and Jean looked at their aunt. "Would you like to ride out to the Hodge home with us this afternoon?" Jean asked.

Miss Dana said she would be delighted to go. "As a matter of fact, I'd like to meet this Miss Mathilde Price," she added.

"That would be wonderful," said Tammi. "Maybe you could tell her to be nice to me."

Tammi was happy they could start right away. Since Louise and Jean were on vacation and had no plans for the afternoon, they were eager to begin their investigation.

"Tammi, you can show us the way," Jean said.

Aunt Harriet and the three girls set off, with Louise behind the wheel. The mountain on which Tammi lived was about three miles out of town.

"Grandpa owned the whole area," Tammi explained as they approached it. "See that house way up near the top? That's our place."

Part of the mountain was wooded. In other sections there were overgrown fields. Tammi said that Grandpa Hodge had spent a great deal of time with experiments in the cellar and did not take care of the land.

"What kind of experiments?" Jean asked.

Tammi said she did not know. Her grandfather

had never invited her to enter his workroom, and she had never bothered to go there herself.

"Maybe," Aunt Harriet spoke up, "your grandfather made a great discovery and wrote about it."

Tammi did not answer. She was looking ahead and finally said to the others, "That's funny. There's the lane leading up the mountain to our house. Somebody has put a barrier across the entrance."

As Louise reached the spot, she stopped the car. Everyone stared at the barrier. Painted across the top of the wooden gate were the words *Positively No Admittance.*

"I wonder if Miss Mathilde had that sign set there," Tammi said, her eyes flashing. "Well, anybody is welcome to my house. I'm going to move the barrier!"

She jumped out and went to turn the gate sideways. At this moment a man drove up in a truck and called out, "Leave that alone!"

"I live here," Tammi told him defiantly. "Did you put that barrier up?"

The man was large and muscular with dark, bristly hair. He scowled. "Never mind who put it up. It's going to stay. So all of you just turn around and leave!"

By this time Louise had stepped out of the car. She asked the man who he was, and what authority he had regarding the Hodge property.

"My name is Zavier Roundtree," the tall man

replied, "and my authority is that I'm a surveyor for the county. We're doing some measuring up here at the mountain, and don't want anybody interfering with our job. Matter of fact, the police authorized us to block off this road."

"Well, I have a right to go to my own house!" Tammi declared. "You can't prevent me from that!"

"You can go," the man said. "Suppose you get into my truck and I'll take you up to the house. The rest of you will have to leave."

Tammi whispered into Louise's ear that she was afraid to go with him. Louise asked her if there was another road to the Hodge home.

"Yes, there's a secret trail," Tammi answered. "We can drive to it." She turned to Mr. Roundtree. "We'll all leave," she told him, and climbed back into the Danas' car with Louise. As they turned around, the girls noticed that the man stood still as if guarding the lane.

"I don't understand this," Jean commented. "Since when can a county surveyor chase people away? This is utterly ridiculous."

"I wonder if Mr. Roundtree was on the level," Louise added. "Maybe he's up to something he doesn't want us to know about."

"Then," Aunt Harriet spoke up, "he'll bear watching."

After driving a few minutes Tammi pointed out the secret trail, which led through overgrown woods. They entered it, but soon Jean suggested that they stop and hide the car. "We can walk the rest of the way."

Tammi agreed this was a good idea. "It's pretty rough going."

Aunt Harriet said, "Suppose I stay here and guard the car. You girls go ahead."

Tammi led the way up the hill. The climb was steep but finally they came within sight of the house. It stood just below the peak of the mountain.

As the girls walked toward it, they heard a piercing scream from inside!

CHAPTER II

The Tree Symbols

LOUISE, Jean, and Tammi raced toward the Hodge house. They burst into the living room through the open front door.

A rough-looking man held a tall, slender woman with gray hair and small brown eyes by her right arm. They were shouting loudly at each other, but the girls could not make out the reason for the argument. When they walked in, the couple stopped and stared at them in surprise.

"Miss Mathilde!" Tammi cried out. "Are you all right? Who is this man?"

"Oh—he—he just came in here and asked me for money. Who are these girls with you?"

"My friends, the Danas. They're detectives," Tammi said.

Louise and Jean wished Tammi had not mentioned their sleuthing. The man stared at them, then suddenly turned and raced out the door.

Miss Mathilde scowled. She did not acknowledge Tammi's introduction or thank the girls for rescuing her from further argument.

Louise spoke. "Tammi, you'd better call the police."

Before Tammi had a chance to comply, Miss Mathilde stepped forward. Her face reddened with anger, and she said icily, "Don't you do anything of the sort, Tammi!"

The girl hesitated, then turned as if to go to the phone. The woman grabbed her and said, "Do as I say!"

Louise and Jean understood why Tammi could not stand her. She was dictatorial, and to the Danas' great surprise, she did not seem to be frightened by her recent experience.

Jean asked, "Why don't you want to report this to the authorities? That man should be arrested for trying to hold you up!"

"I think it is none of your business why I don't want the police," Miss Mathilde snapped. "Who are you, anyway?"

Again Tammi explained that they were sisters who lived in Oak Falls and had solved many mysteries.

"Why do we need them here?" Miss Mathilde asked.

Tammi realized that in her effort to carry out her grandfather's wishes, she had aroused her guardian's suspicions. But she would not admit anything.

"Oh, they're friends of mine," she answered.

The woman looked at the Danas long and hard, then said, "Now if you'll excuse us, Tammi and I have something to talk over."

Tammi burst out, "Oh, I know what it is. You're going to ask me why I went away this afternoon."

Miss Mathilde stood very straight. "You *went* away? You *ran* away! And you probably didn't intend to come back, but thought better of it."

Louise and Jean decided to leave. They were sure Tammi could handle her own problem for the time being.

The two girls said good-bye to Miss Mathilde, then turned to Tammi and winked, as if to say, "We'll be back to help you."

This was natural for the Dana girls. Once they took an assignment, they saw it through, even if it meant danger to themselves at times. Not long ago they had been in many tight situations in a case called *The Hundred-Year Mystery*.

The Danas walked outside and Jean said, "I feel sorry for Tammi. Miss Mathilde is the proverbial dragon lady. She could scare the wits out of anybody."

Louise nodded. "She wasn't very friendly. And she didn't like the idea of our visiting Tammi, that's for sure."

"Why didn't she want the police notified? Just because she has to prove to the world that she's not afraid of anything?"

Louise shrugged. "Who knows? Maybe the fellow was her boyfriend and not an intruder at all."

Jean laughed. "I can't imagine that even Dracula would want to date Miss Mathilde." She changed the subject. "I hope we don't run into Mr. Roundtree again. He's not one of my favourite characters either."

"He seemed to be working at the bottom of the mountain," Louise said. "Why don't we walk up to the top and see if we can pick up any clues?"

"Good idea," Jean replied.

The girls climbed to the peak and looked around in wonder.

"What a marvellous view!" Jean remarked, gazing toward distant hills.

"That's about all there is here." Louise laughed. "No buildings, no trees, no bushes. Not even a wild flower."

The two sisters examined the smooth, even ground. They looked around to see if something had been buried, but there was no mound anywhere. They turned stones and dug here and there with their heels, but discovered nothing suspicious.

Finally Louise sighed. "If Grandpa Hodge hid his duplicate manuscript here, he concealed the spot well."

"I just thought of something," Jean said. "If he buried the copy, why didn't he dig it up after the original was stolen?"

"Maybe he forgot where he put it," Louise said with a chuckle.

Jean shook her head. "The whole thing doesn't make much sense, does it?"

The girls searched for another ten minutes for a possible hiding spot, but to no avail. Finally Louise said, "We'd better go. Aunt Harriet will wonder what happened to us."

"You're right," her sister agreed. "Let's hurry."

The two found the secret trail and went down as fast as they could, avoiding brambles and tree branches that hung low over the path. At last they saw the car.

They stopped short. Aunt Harriet was not in the car, and she was nowhere in sight!

"Something must have happened to her," Louise said, worried.

"We'll have to find her," Jean added, and called, "Aunt Harriet, where are you?"

"Over here," Miss Dana replied. "I discovered something interesting. Come and see it!"

Louise and Jean hurried toward the sound of her voice. They saw their aunt standing near a large tree.

"Look at these," Miss Dana said, pointing to three marks that had been cut into the bark.

The girls came closer and stared at the trunk. About five feet from the ground were the initials J.H. Under them was an equilateral triangle. At the bottom was what appeared to be a drawing of a torn sheet from a book or manuscript. Whatever had been written on it had been obliterated by weather and was not legible.

"What do you think these symbols mean?" Aunt Harriet asked.

Her nieces guessed that the initial H could stand for Hodge. But what was Grandpa Hodge's first name? And had he cut the symbols into the bark?

Louise suggested that the triangle might stand for three equidistant trees. "Let's see if we can find two trees that would complete the triangle," she suggested.

"You mean this tree is part of it?" Jean asked.

"I would think so," Louise replied. "You see those two maples over there? Let's pace the distance between them and this tree. It looks as if it could be the same."

"It'll be difficult because of all the little shrubs and bushes in between," Aunt Harriet said.

"I know. We'll have to do the best we can."

There was silence while Aunt Harriet and the girls measured the number of feet between the two maples and the marked tree.

Jean finished first. "I got about twenty-five feet!" she called out.

"So did I," Louise agreed.

Aunt Harriet obtained the same result. "Now that you've found the perfect triangle, what are you going to do about it?" she asked with a grin.

"That's a good question," Jean admitted.

They stood looking at each other, then at the trees, then at the trampled paths they had made between the points of the triangle.

Suddenly Louise snapped her fingers. "I have an idea!" she said.

CHAPTER III

Amazing Information

"WHAT's your great idea, Louise?" Jean asked.

"I've read," her sister replied, "that in old days pirates used to bring their loot ashore to hide it. In order to find it later, they would pick out three trees in a triangle that was equidistant on each side and bury the treasure in the middle. Let's dig here."

Jean giggled. "With what?" she asked.

Aunt Harriet suggested that they had better go home first and pick up shovels and spades. "Also, you should get Tammi's permission. After all, it's her property."

"I'll phone her," Louise said and the three walked back to the car.

When they reached their house, she called Tammi and told her of the plan. The girl agreed, but before Louise could tell her about the tree markings, Tammi had to hang up because Miss Mathilde had come into the room.

"I'll stay home and start dinner," Aunt Harriet declared. "You two go and dig."

"Okay," Louise said, so she and Jean drove back alone.

First, they paced off the number of feet between the trees again, then found the exact centre. They began to dig, but as time wore on, and the hole became deeper and wider, they felt sure it was in vain.

"If there ever was anything here," Louise said, "it has been removed."

"Perhaps," Jean said, "Grandpa Hodge buried his duplicate manuscript at one time, but then changed his mind and took it away."

"That's a logical guess," her sister agreed. "But the question is, Where did he take it?"

The girls filled in the hole they had made, then went to examine the tree with its three marks again. Could they mean something totally different from the searchers' interpretation?

"Maybe Tammi can help us," Jean said. "As soon as we get home, we'll phone her again."

Louise made a face. "I hope Miss Mathilde Price doesn't answer and refuse to let us talk to Tammi."

"That poor girl," Jean said. "*We must help her!*"

When they reached the house, Louise dialled

the Hodge number. Fortunately Tammi answered.

"Miss Mathilde is out in the yard," she said. "That horrible woman's pulling out flowers and bushes."

"Why would she do a thing like that?"

"To transplant them. She said she was going to change the whole garden. Louise, I can't stand it. She has ruined Grandpa's favorite rosebushes already, and there's no telling what the place will look like when she's through!"

"Oh, dear," Louise said. "I don't understand why she's doing this. It's not a good time to transplant anything right now." Then she changed the subject. "Tammi, what was your grandfather's first name?"

"John," the girl replied. "Why?"

Louise told her about the discovery Aunt Harriet had made in the woods. "Jean and I dug a hole to find out whether the symbols on the tree meant hidden treasure, but we found nothing. If your grandfather buried anything there, he must have dug it up later."

"He never mentioned it to me," Tammi said.

Louise now asked her if anything had happened since the Danas left her.

"Nothing," the girl answered. "Miss Mathilde has been laying down the law, but I haven't paid much attention. Oh-oh, here comes old busybody now. I'll have to hang up."

As Louise and Jean sat talking, trying to figure out what their next move should be, the front door opened and a man called out, "Hi. Anybody home?"

"Uncle Ned!" the girls exclaimed and dashed to the door.

A large man with a florid complexion and bright-blue eyes smiled at them. "Well, how are me hearties?"

"We're great, and how are you?" Jean asked.

Captain Dana laughed. "The salt air keeps me fit as a fiddle." Then he saw his sister coming toward him, and held out his arms.

"Harriet!" he said, and hugged Miss Dana.

"This is a wonderful surprise," Aunt Harriet said. "Now we can have a real family dinner."

During the meal, Louise and Jean brought their uncle up-to-date on the mystery they had been asked to solve. At the end, Louise said to him, "Have you any suggestions as to how we might go about it?"

After some thought, Captain Dana replied, "Have you asked at the library if John Hodge has ever published anything?"

"No, we haven't," Jean answered. "We didn't think of it."

"Then I suggest that in the morning I go down there with you and we'll find out," Uncle Ned said. "If he has written in the past, his publisher ought to be able to give you some information."

When they reached the library the following day, he spoke to the supervisor, Karen Liva.

"I think not," she replied to his question. "But I'll look in the card catalogue and *Books in Print*."

After checking she reported that John Hodge had never published anything, at least not under his own name. "If he used a pseudonym, I'm afraid I can't help you."

Before leaving the building, Louise, Jean, and Uncle Ned decided to look in the index file under "discoveries." There was nothing about John Hodge. Finally they gave up the search and left.

"My next suggestion," said Captain Dana, "is a trip to the courthouse to look at Mr. John Hodge's will."

When they arrived, the clerk, Mark Dunn, greeted Uncle Ned with a big smile. "Well, how are you? I haven't seen you in years!" he said. "Are you still crossing the Atlantic every week?"

"I sure am," Captain Dana replied. "Me and the old *Balaska* are mighty chummy." Then he asked if it would be possible to look at John Hodge's will. The clerk nodded and said he would bring it to them.

After reading it, the Danas knew that Grandpa Hodge had left everything to his only relative, Tammi. The Oak Falls Bank had been instructed to appoint a guardian for her, but there was no mention in his will of Miss Mathilde Price.

"Thanks, Mark," Captain Dana said. "My nieces are friends of Tammi Hodge's and are interested in checking up on a few things."

"Why don't you see Mr. Hunter in the trust department of the Oak Falls Bank?" Mark Dunn suggested. "I'm sure he can tell you more about it."

"Good idea," Captain Dana said. "Thanks."

At the bank, they had to wait until Mr. Hunter was free to meet them. Then they introduced themselves and told him that they were friends of Tammi's.

Louise said, "We have just read Hodge's will and learned that you appointed Tammi's guardian. Would you mind telling us why you chose Miss Mathilde Price?"

Mr. Hunter, a good-looking, red-haired man in his fifties, glanced at them, puzzled. "Why are you asking?"

"Because Tammi doesn't like her," Jean explained. "The two don't get along. Miss Price is very dictatorial and is changing everything in the house and garden. This makes Tammi unhappy because she loved her grandfather dearly and would prefer to have things left just the way he left them."

Mr. Hunter was sympathetic. "I'm sorry to hear that. I didn't know Miss Price personally, but knew she was an old friend of John's. She came to me with a letter from him, in which he mentioned that in case of his death he wanted her to be Tammi's guardian."

Louise and Jean were suspicious. "Did you ever compare the handwriting with that of Mr. Hodge?" she asked.

Mr. Hunter furrowed his brow. "The letter was typed and merely signed 'John Hodge,' " he replied.

The Danas looked at each other. Their thoughts were the same: the letter could be a forgery, and Miss Mathilde Price could have an ulterior motive. Could it have to do with Grandpa Hodge's secret? Had she somehow found out about his discovery?

Mr. Hunter sensed that they doubted the letter had been written by Mr. Hodge. "The signature looked like John's," he said thoughtfully, "but I'll check into the matter. I'll arrange to pay Tammi and Miss Price a visit as soon as I can."

Louise told the executor that the girls had had trouble reaching the Hodge home because the county surveyor had put up a roadblock and would not let them through.

"I never heard of such a thing," Mr. Hunter declared.

"We suspect," Jean said, "that the man is a phony."

"I'll ask if the mountain peak is being surveyed by the county," Mr. Hunter promised. "Did you get the fellow's name?"

"Yes. Zavier Roundtree," Louise replied.

"I've never heard of him," Mr. Hunter said, "but I'll find out if he's telling the truth."

After the Danas had thanked Mr. Hunter and left, Louise said, "I think we should visit Tammi this afternoon."

"Good idea," Jean agreed. "Perhaps we can pick up another clue to what Zavier Roundtree is up to."

The girls dropped off Captain Dana, then drove to the Hodge home. When they reached the lane, Louise noticed that the roadblock was gone.

"Do you think Zavier Roundtree removed it?" she asked.

Jean grinned. "Maybe big strong Zavier is afraid of us!"

"I doubt that," Louise said practically. "And I wonder if we should use this lane or approach the other way."

"Since the barrier is gone, why don't we drive right up?" Jean asked. "Obviously Roundtree finished whatever he was doing and took it away."

"Okay. But keep an eye out for him."

The two girls arrived at the house without seeing anyone. They were surprised to find the front door open.

"How strange!" Jean said, and shouted, "Tammi?" No one answered.

Both had a feeling that something was wrong. They walked into the house, calling Tammi and

Miss Mathilde. They looked in each room, but no one was there. When they reached Tammi's bedroom, the Danas stopped short in utter astonishment. Tammi lay on the floor with her hands and feet tied and a gag in her mouth!

"Tammi!" Jean cried out. "Tammi, what happened to you? Who did this?"

CHAPTER IV

Diary Notation

QUICKLY Louise and Jean loosened the gag and untied the ropes around Tammi's hands and feet. The girl sat up, breathing heavily, then she started to cry.

"You'll be all right," Louise said soothingly. "I'll bring you something to drink, then you can tell us what happened."

She went into the kitchen and returned with a tall glass of soda. Gratefully Tammi gulped down the refreshing drink.

"Oh, that was good," she said. "My mouth was so dry from that gag."

The Danas led Tammi into the living room, where she curled up on the couch. Jean put an arm around her. "You're shivering," she said. "Are you cold?"

Tammi nodded.

"I'll get you a blanket," Jean said and went into the bedroom. She took an eiderdown off Tammi's bed, then wrapped it around the girl.

"Do you feel well enough to tell us what happened?" she asked.

"Yes," Tammi said. "It was awful. Two men whom I had never seen before came here in a car. They had bushy beards and very little of their faces showed."

"What did they say?" Louise asked.

"Nothing. Not a word. But one grabbed Miss Mathilde and held her tight. I ran into my room and tried to lock the door, but the other man was too quick for me. He caught me before I had a chance to do anything and pulled some rope from his pocket."

"And he tied you up," Jean added.

Tammi nodded. "I could see his accomplice holding Miss Mathilde because the door was wide open. They didn't tie her, but dragged her out to the car."

"Then they left?" Jean asked.

"I'm sure the men were planning to come back for me, but they must have seen you approach the house, because suddenly they drove away down a lane on the other side of the mountain."

"Wow! What timing!" Jean exclaimed. "If Louise and I had been a few seconds later, they would have taken you off, too!"

Tammi began to shake. "You—you may have saved my life!"

She looked so frightened that Louise took both her hands into her own. "Oh, Tammi, I think they wanted you both out of this house. But why?"

Jean, deep in thought, furrowed her brow, "I wonder if the kidnapping was just a pretence," she said.

"You mean, Miss Mathilde went with the men voluntarily?" Louise asked.

"It's possible. They didn't tie *her* up. Did they?"

"Oh, but she struggled and screamed," Tammi said. "I don't think she wanted to go with them."

"She might have faked it," Jean said. "The men's beards could have been disguises. Maybe both Tammi and Mathilde knew them, but they didn't want Tammi to recognize them."

"Do you think they'll come back for me?" Tammi asked, her voice shaking.

"If they do, they'll have to contend with us," Jean said. "We won't leave you alone after this."

The Danas now told Tammi what they had learned that morning at the library and the courthouse. "It puts Miss Mathilde in a very suspicious light," Jean said.

"Can you tell us more about Miss Price?" Louise prodded.

Tammi told them that the night before, after

she had gone to bed, she heard a voice. "I realized that Miss Mathilde was on the phone, but her voice was so low I couldn't understand what she was saying. The only thing I caught was 'hurry up.' Do you think she was talking about the kidnapping?"

"It's possible," Jean replied. "But whether she's in with the men or not, one thing is certain. There must be something in this house that they want. Have you any idea what it is?"

Tammi shook her head. "None. What could possibly be here?"

"Suppose we report the kidnapping to the police and then search thoroughly for Grandpa Hodge's duplicate manuscript?" Louise suggested. "It might give us a clue."

"Good idea," Jean agreed. "You don't mind, do you, Tammi?"

"Of course not. I'll help all I can. Let's start with old busybody's bedroom."

The three girls were about to go upstairs when Jean said, "Somebody had better stand watch. I'll take the first turn."

She positioned herself next to a front window, while Louise and Tammi went to the second floor and walked into Miss Mathilde's bedroom. After looking around and finding nothing suspicious, Louise said, "People often hide things under the mattress."

She lifted the one on the bed. Under it lay a book. When Louise pulled it out she read, *Diary*. "I feel nosey looking into this," the girl said to her friend.

Tammi took the diary from her. "We don't know whose it is, but if it belongs to old busybody we'd better read it. As you detectives say, we may get some clues to the mystery."

"You're right," Louise agreed. "Besides, the diary may have belonged to your grandfather."

Tammi opened it, and realized the handwriting was not Grandpa Hodge's. However, she could not say whether it belonged to a man or a woman. There were no dates in the diary. It was just a continuous, rambling story. Most of it did not interest the girls, but suddenly they came to a page on which there was only one item. It said, "I, Mathilde want two things for Christmas. A dog and a diamond engagement ring."

The two girls burst into laughter, then Tammi said, "Do you think it's possible Miss Mathilde wrote this?"

Louise replied that diaries were sometimes like confessions. "I would say she did."

She asked Tammi to look for a sample of Mathilde Price's handwriting among Grandpa Hodge's papers, so they could compare the two.

"Okay," Tammi said.

She hurried to his desk in the first-floor den, but

presently returned, saying she had found no letters from Miss Mathilde.

"If there ever were any, she probably removed them," Louise guessed.

The girls skimmed through the balance of the diary, but noticed nothing to help them solve the mystery. Tammi said, "Oh, I almost forgot to tell you. Grandpa's desk was a shambles. I guess old busybody went through it, all right. I wonder if she took anything."

They returned the diary to its hiding place, then went down to the first floor. They searched the desk and put it back in order.

Just as they finished, Jean came in. "It's your turn, Louise," she said.

The sisters changed places, Louise taking over as guard. Tammi told Jean what she and Louise had discovered and asked, "Where shall we search next?"

Jean suggested Mr. Hodge's bedroom, and they climbed the stairs once more. They searched through John Hodge's drawers and closets, but came across nothing that gave them a clue to the secret of the mountain peak.

On a table lay a large, old-fashioned Bible. Jean opened it, and after turning several pages, called out, "Here's something!"

Tammi hurried to her side and looked at a sheet of paper. "I believe this is the fly leaf of the missing duplicate manuscript!" Jean exclaimed.

It was handwritten in Grandpa Hodge's script and was entitled, *Discovered by John Hodge: The Puma's Treasure.*

"What exactly is a puma?" Tammi asked.

"It's a breed of wild cat," Jean replied.

"Let's hunt for more pages," Tammi urged.

Although they searched thoroughly, the Bible yielded no more clues to the missing manuscript. Jean closed the old book, and the two girls looked at each other. Where should they search next they wondered.

"I know what!" Tammi spoke up. "Grandpa used to spend a lot of time in his basement laboratory. Let's go there."

Jean was intrigued by this idea and followed Tammi to the cellar. When they reached a door marked *Lab*, Tammi opened it and flicked on the light switch. Several pieces of machinery started working simultaneously, making a loud whirring sound.

"Amazing!" Jean exclaimed.

As she stared at the wheels and belts, the young detective wondered aloud if Grandpa Hodge's discovery had anything to do with this room.

"He never told me anything about it," said Tammi.

Just then Louise called down the cellar stairway. "Jean, Tammi, are you there?"

"Yes," Jean replied.

"A car's coming to the house," Louise reported. "You'd better hurry up here."

"Okay," Tammi called, and turned off the light. The two girls closed the door and scooted up the stairs.

CHAPTER V

Night Intruder

THE girls went to a front window and glanced out. Mr. Hunter was standing at the door.

Louise opened it and asked him to come inside. "We're so glad it's you," she said. "We just had some real excitement here."

"What happened?" the kindly man asked, looking worried.

"Two men came in and took Miss Mathilde away," Tammi said. "They tied me up and were about to kidnap me, too, when the Danas arrived and scared them off."

"What!" Mr. Hunter exclaimed. "This is very serious. Tell me all that happened."

When the girls had given him the details, he said, "I wonder if one of the men could have been the surveyor. I checked with the county administration. They have no Zavier Roundtree working for them. When I heard that, I knew trouble was brewing. Yet I drove all around the area without seeing anyone suspicious."

"Zavier Roundtree could have been one of the kidnappers," Louise suggested. "Tammi said they both wore beards, which might have been a disguise."

"Have you any idea why anyone would want Tammi out of this house?" Jean asked the banker.

Mr. Hunter shook his head. "There's nothing unusual about the estate as far as I can see," he said. "Tammi, you don't know where they took Miss Mathilde?"

"No," Tammi replied.

Mr. Hunter went on, "We checked Mr. Hodge's signature on her letter against the one we have on file. It looks so similar, only an expert can tell if it's a forgery. In view of what happened here, I'll turn the matter over to one."

Mr. Hunter glanced around the room. "Tammi, you shouldn't stay alone in this house," he said. "It's too dangerous. If you want, I'll make arrangements—"

"Oh, please don't," Jean spoke up. "We'll take Tammi home with us. We'd love to have her, and she'll be safe with us."

Tammi hugged her. "Oh, will you? I'd love to stay with you." Then she told Mr. Hunter about her grandfather's laboratory in the basement and suggested that he look at it.

"We're sure there's a secret connected with this house, and maybe it has something to do with Grandpa's experiments."

"I'm curious to see it," the banker agreed.

Tammi locked the front door and the group went into the cellar. Mr. Hunter was amazed at the laboratory and the whirring noise of the machinery.

Jean walked ahead of the others to the far side of the room. Suddenly a frayed strip of a fast-moving wide leather belt broke off. It slapped her on the side of the face so hard that she fell to the floor!

"Oh!" Tammi cried out.

Everyone rushed to Jean's side. She lay unconscious on the floor. Louise quickly gave her first aid until she sighed deeply and opened her eyes. She put a hand to her head.

"Oh, what a headache I have," she moaned.

Louise ran to a sink she had noticed and grabbed a towel. She soaked it in cold water, wrung it out, and put it on her sister's face.

"That feels good," Jean said.

Louise renewed the cold compress after a few minutes, then Jean felt better and wanted to get up. The others helped the injured girl to her feet.

"I'd like to go home," she said and managed a wan smile. "I've had enough detective work for today."

"Good idea," Louise agreed.

Tammi turned off the light and everyone went upstairs. They said good-night to Mr. Hunter, then locked the door and drove to the Dana home.

Aunt Harriet and Uncle Ned were startled by their story. Both welcomed Tammi and said she could stay as long as she wished.

"You two are so sweet," Tammi declared and hugged them.

Jean felt better, but wanted to go to bed and rest. Her cheek still stung from being slapped so hard, but her headache was gone.

"I think you should go to bed and rest," Aunt Harriet advised. "I'll bring you something to eat."

"If you want to spoil me, I won't argue," Jean said with a grin. "But really, you don't have to go through all this trouble."

"It's no trouble. Go ahead and I'll be up in a few minutes."

After dinner, Uncle Ned said to Tammi, "I'm worried about leaving your house alone. I think I'll ride up there and look around to be sure your mysterious enemies aren't there."

"Oh, may I come?" Tammi asked eagerly.

"Me, too!" Louise added.

"Why not? I'd rather have company than go by myself."

"Who's going where?" Jean asked. She had just walked through the door in her bathrobe and had overheard the last part of the conversation.

"We're driving to the mountain-peak house to

see if everything is all right," Uncle Ned explained to her.

"I want to join you," Jean declared. "I came down because I'm not tired enough to sleep. Please, Aunt Harriet, I feel fine. May I go with them?"

Miss Dana hesitated. "Well, if you really think you feel up to it—"

"Thanks, Aunt Harriet. I'll run upstairs and put on my clothes. Be back in a minute!"

Soon the group was on their way to the mountain peak. As they neared it, Tammi cried out, "Look! There's a moving light in our living room!"

Captain Dana pulled to the side of the driveway and stopped the car. "You're right!" he said tensely. "We'd better park here and walk up so we won't warn the intruder!"

Silently they climbed out of the car and advanced toward the house. When they peered into the window, they saw a man with a flashlight. He was playing it over the bookshelves along one wall.

"What do you think he's looking for?" Tammi whispered.

"Who knows?" Louise answered. "In any case, he's a burglar!"

Captain Dana agreed and stepped to the front door. He found it unlocked, and the three tiptoed in. Tammi turned on the hall light, then the one in the living room. The intruder, an open book in his hands, whirled and blinked in the bright glare.

"Who are you?" Uncle Ned thundered.

The man stared at him in utter surprise. In order to stall, he answered with a question of his own. "Who are you?"

"I live here," Tammi said. "How did you get in?"

"Oh—eh—I have the key," the man replied. "But I didn't have to use it. The door was open."

"Who gave it to you?" Uncle Ned asked.

"Eh—the bank. Trustee for this property. You see, the house is to be sold, and I'm Ben Rush, an auctioneer. I was asked to dispose of the contents, so I came to see what's here."

"At this time of night?" Uncle Ned asked sarcastically.

"Oh, we're very busy, very busy."

Tammi was greatly upset. "Wait a minute. This house is not for sale. What are you talking about?"

"The bank hasn't informed you yet?" Rush asked. "Well, I'm sure they'll call you in the morning."

Louise did not believe the stranger. She quietly left the room, went to the kitchen, and picked up the local telephone book. She checked under the letter R. No Ben Rush was listed.

"I knew he was lying," the girl told herself. "I'd better call Mr. Hunter." She looked up his home phone number and seconds later had the banker on the line. Quickly she told him what was happening.

"That man's lying!" Mr. Hunter exclaimed. "I'll get in touch with Police Chief Ignari at once. Try to hold the burglar until we get there."

"All right," Louise replied.

She put down the receiver and went back to the living room.

Ben Rush had manoeuvered himself toward the door. "Well, I'd better be going," he said and tried to edge past Louise.

"Oh, no you don't!" she said. "I phoned the executor, and he told me to keep you here until the police arrive. Your story is not true!"

When Rush heard Louise's accusation, he pushed her roughly out of the way and leaped into the hallway. Uncle Ned had anticipated the move and was right on the man's heels.

Rush had not reached the front door yet when Captain Dana tackled him. The girls hurried to his aid and while they put their backs to the door, Uncle Ned held the intruder firmly. Ben Rush could not escape!

"Now," Uncle Ned said sternly to the prisoner, "do you want to tell the truth?"

A sly look came into the man's eyes. With a toss of his head, he said, "I'll tell you if you promise not to have me booked."

Louise reminded him that she and the others were not in charge. "The executor is the person who will decide whether or not you'll be arrested."

Rush pulled away from Captain Dana and sat down in a chair. Although the others plied him with questions, he refused to say another word.

Twenty minutes later Mr. Hunter arrived with two policemen. He introduced them as John Rad and Tom Buxton, and they looked at the girls in amazement.

"It's not every day that three young ladies help catch an intruder," Officer Rad said with admiration.

Louise smiled. "To tell you the truth, we didn't expect to!" She related the story of Rush's capture, then the policemen took the burglar away.

"Mr. Hunter, my house isn't for sale, is it?" Tammi asked, still worried.

"Of course not. It was just something that Ben Rush made up to talk himself out of a tight spot," the banker replied. He turned to Jean. "How do you feel?"

"Much better," Jean replied. "And I'm glad I was able to come along tonight."

"I've been thinking," Mr. Hunter went on, "that we should try to turn off the machinery in the cellar to avoid further accidents."

Uncle Ned nodded. "Let's go down to the lab. I'd like to look at Mr. Hodge's place anyway."

Captain Dana was intrigued when he saw the

complicated apparatus. He and Mr. Hunter searched for an outlet in the wall. They finally found one and Mr. Hunter pulled the plug. The noisy whirring sounds stopped, and a few minutes later everyone went back upstairs.

Before Mr. Hunter left, he looked at Tammi. "I almost forgot. I have some good news for you," he said.

CHAPTER VI

Important Scraps

TAMMI's eyes lit up. "What is it?" she asked eagerly.

"I realize the school you have been attending up to now does not go beyond the eighth grade. Since you are entering high school next year, you will have to transfer. I have chosen one where I know you'll be happy, the Starhurst School for Girls in Penfield."

Louise cried out, "That's the school Jean and I attend. We love it! Tammi, you'll be happy there."

"How wonderful!" Tammi exclaimed. "And I'll have friends!" She thanked Mr. Hunter for arranging the nice surprise.

When the excitement died down, Uncle Ned said, "This house should not be left unguarded. Suppose I get a detective to stay here?"

The executor of the Hodge estate thought this

was a good idea. "You know someone you could ask?"

"I'll check with Chief Ignari. Maybe he can help us."

The chief promised to assign a plainclothesman who would bring along his dog for extra protection. Then he asked, "Captain Dana, could you and the girls stay at the mountain peak until the officer arrives?"

"We'll be glad to," Uncle Ned replied. "Have you had a chance to speak to the prisoner yet?"

"Yes," the chief said. "But he isn't talking. Of course, he's entitled to speak to a lawyer first, and he knows it. He'll see one tomorrow."

"I hope he changes his mind and tells us what he was looking for," Uncle Ned said. "By the way, would you please instruct the detective who will come here not to admit Miss Mathilde Price to the house if she should show up?"

The chief agreed and Uncle Ned put down the phone.

At about eleven o'clock the detective arrived. He introduced himself as Mr. Fife, and his beautiful German shepherd as Homer.

"He's well trained but not vicious," Mr. Fife explained. "He won't harm you once he knows you're friends of mine."

The girls fell in love with the intelligent animal at once. They patted and talked to him. Homer, who initially had looked questioningly at his master, soon was licking their hands and playing with them.

Mr. Fife smiled. "I can see you won't have any trouble with him. Will you be back tomorrow? I can stay only at night."

"Yes," Louise replied. "If you'll guard the house overnight, we'll take care of it in the daytime."

The girls drove off with Captain Dana. On the way he said, "I didn't realize we would be staying at the Hodge house so long. I must catch a midnight plane for New York and get back to the *Balaska*. Tell your Aunt Harriet I said good-bye. I'll be home again soon."

Louise dropped her uncle off at the Oak Falls airport, then she, Jean, and Tammi drove home. By the time they reached the Dana house, Tammi was extremely tired. When Aunt Harriet saw this, she put her arms around the girl. Tammi began to cry, and for the first time really broke down and sobbed over the loss of her grandfather.

Between the tears, however, she kept saying how fortunate she was to have found such wonderful friends. Aunt Harriet left the living room but presently came back with some warm milk and toast.

"Drink this, dear," she said. "Then take a warm bath and we'll tuck you into bed. I'm sure you'll sleep like a kitten."

As soon as Tammi had finished the midnight repast, she went upstairs with Aunt Harriet and a little while later, as predicted, she was sound asleep.

Next morning Tammi felt fine, and Jean declared she had completely recovered although she did have a bruise on the side of her face. The telephone rang, and Louise answered it.

The caller was Mr. Fife. "Please come here as soon as you can," he said. "I have received word of a special assignment I must take care of for the police department."

He then told Louise that Homer, who had been left on watch outside the house during the night, had barked loudly twice and raced off after intruders on the property.

"I don't know whether they were humans or animals," Mr. Fife said. "But after the trouble here, I'm inclined to think that they were people. I guess you won't have anything to worry about. Homer seems to understand what he's to do."

Louise repeated the conversation to Aunt Harriet and the girls, who agreed to leave at once. Cora Appel, their day worker, whom Jean had nicknamed Applecore, would come later to take care of the cleaning.

"We'll just leave everything," Miss Dana said, "and I'll write Cora a note."

When she and the girls reached Tammi's home, Mr. Fife quickly said good morning, then walked out the door. Homer did not make an attempt to follow when his master drove away.

"He is well trained," Jean remarked, and hugged the beautiful animal.

Louise nodded, then said, "I suggest we start hunting for clues right away. We've already searched Miss Mathilde's and Grandpa Hodge's rooms, so where do you want to go next?"

"How about the den?" Tammi suggested. "We went through the desk, but haven't really checked out the rest of the place."

The Danas agreed and followed Tammi into the den.

As they looked around, Jean suddenly said, "This is funny. With all the cleaning and re-arranging Miss Mathilde did, there are still ripped-up papers in the wastebasket."

"I suppose she never bothered to empty it," Tammi said. "And to tell you the truth, I didn't even notice the basket myself, because it was underneath the desk."

Jean turned it over on the floor. "Maybe we can piece some of these scraps together. Here. This looks interesting. It's obviously part of a letter written to the American Archeological Society because it has the address on it."

After a good deal of work, the girls reconstructed the letter. In it, Grandpa Hodge promised he would have his manuscript ready by April.

"But it was obviously stolen before then," Tammi said.

The letter appeared to be a carbon copy and was not signed. In the lower left corner were the initials JH/ML.

Jean continued to fit other pieces together and wondered who ML was. A few minutes later she had reconstructed a scribbled note to a Mary Lyon.

"Tammi," she asked, "do you know who Mary Lyon is?"

"Yes," the girl replied. "She did secretarial work for Grandpa."

"I believe we've picked up a wonderful clue," Jean said. "Where does she live?"

"In Woodstock," Tammi replied, and everyone was eager to talk to Mary Lyon.

"I'll call her," Tammi offered, as she went to the phone.

She explained to her grandfather's former secretary that she was investigating the estate with the Dana girls, and that they would like to have some information about Mr. Hodge's work.

The Danas stood close enough to hear Mrs. Lyon's reply. "I might be able to help you, Tammi, but I don't want to discuss it over the phone. Can you and your friends come here to see me?"

Tammi looked at Louise and Jean. Both nodded. "Yes," she said into the telephone. "We'll be there in a little while."

"Shall we all go?" Louise asked.

"I don't think that's such a good idea," Aunt

Harriet objected. "Why don't you take Tammi? Jean and I will stay here and guard the house."

Everyone agreed and the two girls got their hand-bags. They said good-bye and drove off. At the foot of the hill Louise noticed a green sedan parked a short distance from the lane.

Tammi paid no attention to it, but Louise looked intently at the driver when she passed him. "I believe that's Zavier Roundtree," she thought uneasily.

She turned into the main road, but watched the suspect in the rearview mirror. To her dismay, he followed her!

CHAPTER VII

The Doodler

For a couple of miles Tammi did not understand why Louise kept looking in the rearview mirror to watch the green sedan behind her. Finally she turned around, however, and glanced out the window.

"Do you think that man is following us?" she asked, worried.

"I'm afraid so," Louise replied. "I think he's Zavier Roundtree."

Tammi was alarmed. "What are we going to do?" she said. "He'll harm us!"

Louise did not comment but silently agreed with Tammi. The man might come alongside and force them off the road!

Suddenly Tammi jumped up and down in the seat and cried, "Go faster, Louise! Don't let that guy catch us!"

Louise put on speed. So did the car following her. How could she shake the driver?

Just then she passed a sign for a large shopping mall about half a mile ahead. A sudden idea came to Louise. "I think I know how to get rid of that man," she told Tammi.

"How?"

"You see the shopping mall ahead? Maybe we can lose him in there." Louise pulled into the entrance and went past the last line of cars. Then she turned right and drove up the next aisle. Her pursuer did the same.

When Louise reached the end, she turned left and scooted into the next lane. Halfway down a woman suddenly backed out in front of her without looking in either direction. Louise jammed on the brakes, which squealed loudly, and avoided hitting the car by inches.

The girls felt frustrated. Their pursuer was already turning down the aisle after them. Fortunately the woman pulled back into her parking slot and the girls shot past her. Tammi looked back through the rear window and exclaimed, "Oh, that lady is backing out again!"

She closed her eyes, waiting for a crash, but the man in the green sedan hit his brakes and stopped the car just in time to avoid colliding with the woman.

Louise realized she had the advantage now and

hurried to the end of the aisle, turned left, and drove out a side exit onto another road.

Tammi's eyes were still glued to the window. "I guess the lady backed all the way out this time," she cried. "I see her coming down the lane right now. But there's no sign of the green sedan!"

Louise laughed. "I suppose we can thank that woman for letting us get away."

Tammi wanted to know where they were.

"I'm not sure," Louise replied. "I'll stop at the next petrol station and ask for directions."

She did, and an attendant told her how to get to Woodstock. When they reached the town, Louise followed the directions Mary Lyon had given them, and found her house without trouble.

She opened the door and swooped Tammi into her arms. "How glad I am to see you, my dear!" she exclaimed.

"I'm happy to see you, too," Tammi replied. "Mrs. Lyon, this is my friend Louise Dana. She's a detective."

Mary Lyon laughed. "I'm delighted to meet you, Louise. I've never spoken to a real live detective—especially a girl!"

Louise assured her that she was only an amateur, but that she and her sister loved to solve mysteries. "I do hope you can help us with the one involving Grandpa Hodge," she added.

Mary Lyon was middle-aged and pleasant looking. She told Louise that after her husband had passed away and her children had married and left home, she had gone to work on a part-time basis for Grandpa Hodge.

"He was a brilliant man," she said. "But I admit that at times I didn't understand what he was talking about."

Louise asked her if she had ever helped him with a manuscript.

"No," Mary Lyon replied. "Mr. Hodge was a rather secretive man."

Tammi spoke up. "Well, Grandpa told me it had been stolen, and I was to get the Dana girls to help me find the duplicate."

"That's very interesting," Mary Lyon said. "Have you had any luck?"

"No," Tammi replied. "And besides, we've had plenty of trouble. The executor sent an awful woman to take care of me. Her name is Miss Mathilde Price, and she's a real pain. She got kidnapped, and I'm glad!"

"Kidnapped?" Mrs. Lyon repeated in surprise.

"That's right," Tammi replied. "Now I'm staying with the Danas, and in the fall I'm going to Starhurst with them."

"I'm glad to hear that," Mrs. Lyon said. "But please tell me the whole story from the beginning, and I'll see if I can fill in any pieces of the puzzle."

Louise gave her full details from the time Tammi

had come to their house with her request. Mary Lyon was surprised to hear that Mr. Hodge had any enemies.

"He was a kind, gentle person, and never mentioned any difficulties with other people. Once he told me he had made a discovery and was writing a book. But he never asked me to type any of it."

"Have you any idea what the discovery might have been?" Louise inquired.

The woman shrugged. "Perhaps it had something to do with digging. Once, when I was to go to his home, I arrived early. No one was in the house, so I sat in the car and waited for him. After a while, Mr. Hodge came from the opposite direction. He was carrying a shovel and his shoes were muddy."

Louise was excited by this information, but sorry that Mary Lyon could not tell her where the elderly man had been digging.

"He subscribed to a magazine about stars," Mrs. Lyon went on. "Whenever there were charts he used to draw lines from one star to another, making triangles and other geometric figures. He was a real doodler. Often he seemed to be dissatisfied with his work and would rub it out."

Mrs. Lyon smiled. "I used to find pieces of paper on which he had drawn a series of triangles. Is this information helpful to you?"

Louise said she was not sure, but told Mrs.

Lyon about the three equidistant trees in the woods and the strange markings on one of them.

"At the top were the initials J.H., which we assume stand for John Hodge. Below them was a triangle, and under that the drawing of what might have been a page torn from a manuscript."

"How strange!" the ex-secretary exclaimed. "I'm sorry I can't help you on that, either. As I told you before, Mr. Hodge was a very secretive man."

She wished the girls luck in solving the mystery and promised to call them if she thought of anything else that might be helpful. Louise gave her the Danas' number, then they said good-bye and drove off.

When they reached the foot of the lane leading up to the mountain-peak home, Tammi suddenly put a hand on Louise's right arm. "Slow down for a moment. There's a package under that tree just ahead."

Louise stopped the car before turning into the lane.

"I'll get it," Tammi offered and opened the door.

"No!" Louise warned her. "Do you realize that package is at the very same spot where Zavier Roundtree's car was standing before he followed us?"

"You mean he might have lost it?" Tammi asked, hesitating.

"Either that, or he could have put it there on purpose."

"But why?"

"For us to pick up. Tammi, there might be something dangerous in that package—a bomb, for instance!"

CHAPTER VIII

Vicious Dogs

TAMMI turned white. "A bomb!" she cried out. "You don't really believe that?"

Louise looked thoughtful. "I really don't know. All I know is we shouldn't take any chances."

"What'll we do, then?" Tammi asked. "Call the police?"

Louise nodded. "Why don't you run up to the house and ask Aunt Harriet to phone them. I'll stay here and watch the package."

"All right. But you'd better not go close to it in case it is what you think."

"Don't worry. I'll sit right here in the car," Louise assured her.

Tammi scooted off. While Louise waited in the car, she began to have misgivings about the package. Maybe there was nothing explosive in it, and she would feel foolish in front of the police!

Just then a station wagon came along the road.

As it drew near, Louise noticed that a woman was driving and that she had a number of children with her. A little girl who was looking out the window suddenly cried, "Mummy, Mummy, stop! See that package over there? Priscilla said I'd find a surprise today. Maybe it's my surprise!"

The woman laughed and pulled over to the side. "It won't be your surprise, Karen, but we'll see what's in it anyway."

"Oh, yes, let's see the surprise," a little boy squealed and opened the door of the station wagon.

As the children and their mother proceeded to climb out, Louise hurried over to them.

"Please don't touch that package!" she warned. "My friend and I are afraid it's a bomb. We're waiting for the police."

"What?" the woman looked at her incredulously. "Whatever gave you that idea?"

"I know the man who dropped it. He's trying to harm us."

"Did you watch him put it there?"

"No. But his car stood at the same spot not long ago."

"You must be imagining things. I'm picking up the box and checking what's inside."

"Please, don't," Louise pleaded. "If my suspicions are correct, you—"

"Aw, come on. You probably want the package for yourself."

Louise was annoyed. "If that was the case, I could have picked it up long before you arrived on the scene," she said. "And I don't have a car full of children who might get hurt!"

The argumentative woman finally gave in. "Oh, all right. Come on, kids, let's get back into the car!" The children were reluctant to leave the strange box, but their mother insisted. Without thanking Louise for possibly saving her and the youngsters from a bad accident, she climbed behind the wheel and drove off.

Louise sighed in relief. A few minutes later two policemen pulled up. They eyed the package, then asked Louise why she was suspicious.

The girl detective told them about the man who had been parked at the spot earlier, who, she thought, was Zavier Roundtree. "I wasn't sure enough at first to report him, but now I am because he followed us. I had Tammi Hodge in the car with me and didn't want anything to happen to her, so I figured out a way to shake the man. It worked."

One of the officers, who carried a tool kit, said he was an explosives expert. He walked over to the package and took a number of gadgets from his box. First he held one of them up to the package, then another.

Finally he said, "I don't think it's a bomb. Let's open it."

Louise felt sheepish, but two minutes later she

changed her mind. The package was filled with bottles. The officer took off the caps one by one and smelled the liquids inside.

He frowned. "They're various deadly acids," he declared. "If taken internally, any one of them could kill a person or cause a severe burn if it comes in contact with the skin."

"How awful!" Louise exclaimed. "Please take them with you. I hope you find Zavier Roundtree, because I'm sure he left the package, hoping to harm Tammi and the rest of us."

"We'll work on it," the bomb expert promised. "The department will also alert the state police and ask them to help keep this area under surveillance. Roundtree may return to see if the package is gone."

The officers drove off, and Louise continued to the Hodge house. When she told Aunt Harriet, Jean, and Tammi what had happened, Miss Dana said in relief, "It's a good thing you were suspicious of that package. I feel better having the police doubling their efforts in this area."

During supper the phone rang. Tammi answered it. "Miss Mathilde?" she asked, then motioned for the others at the table to come and overhear what was being said.

"I'm a prisoner," the woman on the other end told her. "But I hope to be released soon. I'm terribly worried about you, Tammi. Are you all right?"

"I'm fine," Tammi replied. "My friends, the Danas, are taking me to their house every night, while a detective guards this place with his big police dog. The Danas and I come back in the morning and stay during the day."

The woman did not answer, and Jean whispered in Tammi's ear, "Ask her where she is."

Tammi did, but the caller hung up abruptly. The girl looked puzzled.

Aunt Harriet asked, "Are you sure that was Miss Mathilde?"

"Yes, it sounded just like her."

"Obviously," Louise said, "her phony kidnappers made her call to find out what's going on here."

Tammi was embarrassed. "I suppose I shouldn't have told her anything."

The Danas agreed but said nothing. They did not want to upset Tammi any more than she already was.

"Don't worry," Jean advised. "Just imagine, if Miss Mathilde's kidnappers were planning to come to the house, they won't dare now because they know the place is well guarded."

Tammi sighed. "I hope they never had any such plans. Things are scary enough as it is."

Just then Homer began to bark wildly. The girls rushed outside to see why and noticed two small boys walking toward the house some distance away.

"Can we help you?" Louise called out.

The boys stopped, and one of them replied, "We're selling cookies for our club. Would you like some? But you have to hold your dog."

"Okay," Jean said and grabbed Homer by his collar. "Just don't come any closer."

Aunt Harriet went into the house for money. She gave it to Tammi and told her to pick out something.

Tammi walked up to the boys and selected one box of vanilla and one box of chocolate. The taller of the boys said, "We just saw a man with a dog like yours, only bigger."

"Where was he?" Tammi asked.

"On the road near your lane," the boy replied. "He had the dog on a leash that was really a chain and he told us not to come near, otherwise the dog would attack us."

"You'd better be careful," Tammi advised the boys, then they said good-bye and left.

Tammi returned to the house, and told the Danas what the boy had said, while Jean opened the box of chocolate cookies.

"I don't like the sound of it," Aunt Harriet remarked. "I wonder if the man brought the dog here for exercise, or—"

At that moment they all heard Homer growl. They rushed to the window and looked out.

"Oh, no!" Louise cried.

A large, vicious dog was attacking Homer. Tammi and the Danas hurried outside.

"Stop! Stop!" Aunt Harriet ordered the animals.

They paid no attention. They were snarling, yelping, and biting each other. Louise recalled what the little boy had told her. No doubt this was the dog he had seen. But where was his owner?

She looked around. Half-hidden behind the trees she spotted a strange man holding a chain. "Please take your dog away!" Louise screamed. He paid no attention.

Meanwhile, Jean frantically tried to figure out a way to stop the fight. "Tammi," she cried, "we'll have to do something, or Homer will get hurt!"

"I know," Tammi said. "But what?"

"Maybe they'll stop if we spray them with water. Is there a hose around?"

"Yes. It's rolled beside the house. I'll get it."

Tammi raced off and Jean followed. The hose was connected to an outdoor tap. Tammi turned the water on full force, while Jean grabbed the hose and ran forward with it. She aimed the stream at the two German shepherds.

The animals paid little attention to it and kept on snarling and biting. Jean adjusted the nozzle to get a thinner but stronger stream. However, the only effect it had was to make the dogs turn around so the water hit the backs of their heads instead of their eyes.

"It won't work!" Jean cried out in dismay. "Tammi, you may as well turn the water off."

Tammi did, then ran up to her friend. "What

are we going to do? Look, they're biting each other worse than ever!"

Aunt Harriet had an idea. "Perhaps they'll react to noise," she said and ran into the house. In the kitchen she grabbed two saucepans and hurried outside again. Banging the pans loudly together, she approached the dogs.

The noise startled Tammi and Jean, but the animals paid no attention. The killing fight went on!

CHAPTER IX

False Stairway

THE ugly dogfight continued, and Miss Dana, Jean, and Tammi were unable to stop it. Meanwhile, Louise approached the man from behind the trees, but was afraid to go too near since he held the chain in his hand. If she confronted him, he might use it to scare her or even to hit her!

Suddenly he dropped the chain carelessly and walked a few steps toward the house to get a better view of the fight. Louise sneaked up behind him and quickly picked up the chain. Then she cried out in a loud voice, "Call off your dog!"

The man, whom she had never seen before, whirled. Taken off guard, he stared at Louise, who swung the chain menacingly.

"Call off that dog at once!" she repeated her command. "Or you'll be in trouble with the police!"

The man seemed frustrated, but apparently he

realized that Louise and her friends were serious. He stepped out from behind the trees into the open and whistled for his dog.

At first the two animals, who were engaged in the deadly combat, ignored him. The owner of the strange dog continued to whistle, louder and louder, then he clapped his hands. At the same time, Louise rattled the chain.

Finally the German shepherd heard the insistent summons. He growled and lunged at his opponent one more time, then ran off to his master. He barked at Louise and made a move to approach her, but his owner held him back by the collar.

"Give me my chain!" he called to the girl.

"Oh, no. You'll have to do without it," Louise replied. "Ncw get out of here! Who sent you, anyway?"

Over his shoulder, the stranger retorted, "None of your business!"

Louise stood motionless for a moment, her mind racing. Was he part of Zavier Roundtree's gang? Had he hoped that by killing or incapacitating Homer, he could gain access to the house?

"If I follow him, perhaps I can see what car he's driving and get the license number," the girl told herself. "I'm sure he didn't come on foot this far."

Louise saw the stranger disappear behind a tree and quickly went after him. She tried to walk as quietly as possible so as not to alert the man, and stopped here and there to listen to his footsteps. Suddenly her foot caught in a vine and she crashed headlong to the ground!

"Oh!" she cried out as thorns penetrated her skin. She sat up and looked at her scratched legs and arms. Then she heard a thrashing noise ahead of her.

"No doubt he knows I'm on his trail and he's running with the dog," she thought, frustrated. She got back to her feet and hurried after her quarry, but she had not yet reached the bottom of the hill when a car was started and pulled out of the lane. All Louise could see was the colour, green. She was not close enough to distinguish the make or the licence number.

She bit her lip in disgust. "If only I hadn't fallen!" she thought, and started to walk up the mountain again.

Soon she entered the Hodge house. Tammi stared at her with wide-open eyes. "Your legs are bleeding!" she cried out. "What happened?"

"I tried to follow that man, but my foot got caught and I fell," Louise reported. "He drove off in a green car. How's Homer?"

Tammi had examined Mr. Fife's dog. His back was bleeding in several places where the other dog had nipped the flesh. Otherwise he seemed to be all right, but extremely weary. He lay down and licked his wounds.

"You're a brave dog," Tammi told him, patting his shoulders and neck.

The others left him lying in a quiet spot, where he could sleep and recover from his challenging encounter. Then they discussed what had happened. Obviously it had been another attempt by their enemies to harass and frighten them.

Finally Jean changed the subject. She reminded the others that they had not fully investigated the cellar. "Let's go down now," she suggested.

Aunt Harriet said she would stay upstairs in case anyone should drop by or call on the phone. Since Tammi said there was no electricity except at the bottom of the stairs and in the lab, the girls took flashlights and went to the cellar.

For the first time they noticed that the part beyond the lab door was full of cobwebs and old newspapers. A wooden stairway stood against the far wall.

Jean stared at it in wonder. "There's no indication that there ever was a door at the top," she said. "It doesn't make sense."

"I know," Tammi said. "I asked Grandpa about it once, and he said the stairway didn't lead anywhere. It was just there and he never bothered to remove it."

Since the light was dim, Louise and Jean played their flashlights on the structure for a long time. It was totally enclosed with solid sides and a back piece.

"Maybe it's just standing against the wall without being connected to it," Jean said. "Let's try to move it."

The three girls tugged and yanked, but the structure did not budge.

"I suppose it's attached to the wall after all," Tammi said. "It looks as if this staircase will never come loose."

"Let's not give up yet," Louise decided. "One, two, three, go!"

The Danas and Tammi pulled with all their might. Did they imagine it, or had the stairway come loose a little bit?

"Let's try again," Louise urged. "Ready? One, two, three!"

This time they yanked the old stairway with such force that it suddenly tore off! It tumbled to one side, knocking the girls to the floor!

Jean had been thrown clear of the wooden structure, but Tammi was partially buried and Louise's leg was caught. Slowly Jean sat up, rubbing her neck. She looked at her sister. "Louise, are you all right?"

"I think so, but I can't get my leg out from under this step. Please help me."

Jean lifted the corner of the staircase just enough so Louise could extricate herself.

"Thank goodness," she said and stood up. "I'm sure I haven't any broken bones, but my leg is bruised."

"We must get Tammi out," Jean urged. "She seems to have fainted!"

Just then the girls heard their Aunt Harriet calling from the kitchen, "What happened?"

"We had an accident," Jean replied. "Quick, help us!"

Miss Dana ran down and stared in horror. "Oh, dear, what's the matter with Tammi?"

"We don't know. Can you pull her out while we try to pick up this staircase? It's heavy, but I think we can manage between the two of us."

"Go ahead."

Jean and Louise bent down and lifted the structure. They found to their great relief that it was not resting heavily on Tammi. They had no trouble moving it enough so Aunt Harriet could reach the girl and drag her out. Tammi had a gash on her head, which was bleeding, but she was breathing normally and her eyelids fluttered.

"Are you all right?" Jean asked as she bent over the girl.

Tammi opened her eyes and sat up slowly. "My head hurts," she mumbled.

"You may have broken a bone," Louise said. "Try to stretch your limbs and see if you can stand up."

Tammi nodded. With the help of the Danas, she got to her feet. "I ache all over," she said, "but I don't think it's anything serious."

"Can you walk upstairs if we help you?"

"I think so."

The Danas took Tammi into the living room. Aunt Harriet rushed for a towel and soaked it in cold water, while Louise brought antiseptic and gauze pads with adhesive. The cut in Tammi's head was long, but not deep, and the girls managed to stop the bleeding quickly.

"I think we should take you to the hospital emergency room to see if you need stitches," Aunt Harriet said.

"Oh, please, I'm all right," Tammi insisted. "It doesn't even hurt any more. I want to stay here and just rest for a while."

Miss Dana relented and Tammi said to Louise and Jean, "You must go back to the cellar and see what's behind the staircase. I can't wait to hear what you'll discover."

"Okay," Jean said. "Try to get some sleep while we check out the basement."

The girls went downstairs again, and hurried to the fallen stairway. It was easy to see where it had torn away from the wall.

"Louise!" exclaimed Jean, "There's a door! It was hidden by the stairway."

She beamed her flashlight on it, looking for a knob. Finally she found one. It was so small and well disguised, it was barely visible.

Louise turned the knob, but it would not budge.

"Maybe the door is just a fake," she said. "If it's real, the hinges are on the other side, so we can't work on them."

"Let me check the knob," Jean requested. She turned it right and left. Nothing happened.

"Why don't we pull the door?" Louise urged.

"But no more accidents," Jean begged. "Let's be very careful so it doesn't knock us down."

After yanking on the knob several times the girls realized that the hinges were not giving.

Jean, who admitted that her arms were aching, said with a sigh, "Let's try pushing it open. And after all this trouble, there'd better be something on the other side!"

Louise, whose shoulders hurt too from the arduous pulling, said, "We may find nothing but a lot of old canning jars. Let's go! One, two, three, push!" With a tremendous cracking sound the door gave way, banging against the wall. Behind it was total blackness.

Louise and Jean beamed their flashlights ahead. "This place looks ancient," Jean remarked.

The passageway on the other side of the door had side walls and a ceiling of stone, but the floor was covered with a fine powder.

"That's strange-looking stuff," Jean said. "I wonder what it is."

Louise leaned down to sniff the grayish-white dust. It had no odour.

"I wonder if this could be Grandpa Hodge's secret?" she said.

Jean agreed that this was possible. "He had it well hidden," she replied.

Louise suggested that they go for a pail and shovel and scoop up some of the mysterious powder. "We can take it to a chemist for examination."

"Good idea," Jean agreed.

As the girls reached the kitchen stairway, they heard Homer barking. Jean glanced at her wristwatch. "It's probably Mr. Fife driving up. He's due about now."

"I don't think we should let him in on the secret," Louise said. "I'll run back and close that door." She did, and shortly joined her sister in the kitchen. They were met by Aunt Harriet, and quickly told her what they had found.

"Please wait until tomorrow before collecting any of it," Miss Dana said. "I think we should take Tammi to the doctor. She has a dreadful headache."

Just then Mr. Fife walked in the door. He was visibly disturbed. "I saw Homer," he said. "He looks as if he's been in a fight. Did you have trouble here?"

Louise explained what had happened.

Mr. Fife was incensed. "I'm sure this was done deliberately," he fumed. "Too bad we don't know who the fellow was. Did anyone see if the strange dog had a licence tag, and what the number was?"

Louise shook her head. "We didn't dare get close enough. The animal was ferocious."

Mr. Fife nodded. "It's just as well you didn't go near him. He might have hurt you seriously."

The Danas and Tammi said good-bye to the detective and left. After they reached the main road, Louise said, "We've found something very interesting in the cellar."

"What is it?" Tammi asked.

"There's a passageway behind the spot where those stairs were," Jean told her, "and the floor is covered with a gray-white powder."

"Do you think it has something to do with Grandpa's secret?"

"It could have," Louise said. "Maybe we'll find out tomorrow!"

CHAPTER X

The Strange Powder

ON THE way home, Aunt Harriet and the girls stopped at the doctor's office. Fortunately he was able to examine Tammi at once. He confirmed the fact that she had had a bad bang, but that the cut was not deep.

Smiling, he said, "Tammi, you're a lucky young lady. I'm sure that a good night's sleep will fix you up." He gave her a couple of tablets to take and suggested a light supper.

The following morning the injured girl insisted that she felt fine and wanted to accompany the Danas to her mountain home.

"All right," Aunt Harriet agreed. "But you must all be more careful. We don't want any more trouble."

The girls promised. Then Louise and Jean brought three shovels and buckets from the garage.

"I think we should take a plastic bag, too," Louise said, and went to get one.

When they reached Tammi's home, they said good morning to Mr. Fife and asked if anything exciting had happened during the night.

"I don't know that you'd call it exciting," he replied. "Two phone calls came for Miss Mathilde Price, one from a woman, the other from a man. When I said she wasn't here, both wanted to know who I was. I merely said I was spending the night here, without going into any details."

"I'm glad to hear that," Aunt Harriet said. "It might forestall more trouble."

Louise remarked, "I wonder if the calls were legitimate, or if the gang was trying to get some information."

The detective thought the latter was probably the answer. "I didn't like the tone of voice of either the man or the woman. They weren't a bit friendly."

He went on to say that Homer, who had been on watch outside, had barked loudly during the night. "I checked to see what was worrying him, and both times I noticed flashlights moving down the driveway. The first incident occurred at two o'clock, the other at four—not exactly visiting hours."

"Who do you suppose the intruders were?" Louise asked. "Miss Mathilde's kidnappers?"

"It could even have been the woman herself," Jean replied.

"Do you think they wanted to get something from the house?" Tammi spoke up.

"Maybe they were trying to find out what part of the house I was in," Mr. Fife said. "If it was the gang who made the phone calls, they learned the house was guarded, and they might have wanted to know how well."

Jean sighed. "So many questions and no answers."

Mr. Fife nodded. "Now I'll have to run. See you tonight."

After he left, Louise suggested that the girls go out and see if the intruders had left any clues.

"What do you expect to find, a flashlight battery?" Jean teased.

"Who knows? A good detective leaves no stone unturned," her sister declared, and they went outside.

They spread out and walked down the driveway, scanning the ground carefully.

After a few minutes, Louise called out, "Hey, I found something!" She bent down and picked up a small object. Tammi and Jean ran to her side.

"What is it?" Tammi asked excitedly.

"A red pencil. It has a good point on it, too," Louise replied.

"Oh!" Tammi laughed. "That belongs to me. I've been looking for it all over the house for several days."

"Too bad," Louise said, disappointed. "Well, it was a good try."

The girls continued their search, but had no success. Finally Louise said, "It's no use. Why don't we investigate the secret passageway instead?"

Tammi and Jean agreed. They took the pails, shovels, and plastic bag and descended into the cellar. Tammi, astounded to see the gray-white powder, asked the Danas how they were going to determine what it was.

Louise replied, "We'll take it to a chemist. A good friend of Uncle Ned's who's the head of a chemical company in Oak Falls might be able to help us."

The girls dug up a quantity of the powder and sealed it in the bag. Then Jean said she wanted to investigate the passageway farther along. The three walked over the powder, beaming their flashlights around the interior. It proved to be a long, straight tunnel, which came to a dead end.

"This place is a mystery," said Louise. "I—" she sneezed.

A moment later Jean sneezed, too. "We'd better turn back," she said, beginning to cough. "This stuff is getting to us."

Tammi was already walking toward the entrance. She, too, sneezed and coughed before they were halfway back to their starting point.

When the three girls finally arrived at the first

floor of the house, Aunt Harriet looked at them in dismay. "What in the world happened to you?" she asked, as they continued to sneeze and cough.

"We—" Louise began. Jean added, "walked through—" but she had to cough again.

Tammi said, "The gray-white dust—"

Aunt Harriet did not wait to hear any more. She asked Tammi if there was anything in the house that could be used as a spray for the girls' noses and throats.

Tammi nodded, and through her streaming eyes led Aunt Harriet to a medicine cabinet. She picked out eyedrops, nasal spray, and a gargle. Each girl used them and finally recovered.

Jean giggled. "I haven't cried so much since I was little."

"Nor I," Louise added.

Tammi asked if they could go to town right away to find out what the gray-white powder was. Louise explained to Aunt Harriet about consulting the chemist.

"That's a good idea," Miss Dana agreed. "But I think Tammi should stay here. There is no need for all of you to go, and after her bang on the head yesterday and now this sneezing and coughing, she'd better take it easy."

Tammi was disappointed, but managed a smile. "It's wonderful to have someone worrying about me," she said. "Aunt Harriet, you're just the dearest person in the world. I guess you shouldn't stay alone anyway, even with Homer to protect you."

Louise and Jean drove off. Half an hour later they arrived at the Newstead Company, which was on the outskirts of Oak Falls. When they entered the lobby, Louise asked the receptionist if they could see Mr. Harvey Windsor.

"Who shall I say is calling?" the woman inquired.

"Louise and Jean Dana. Our Uncle Ned is a friend of Mr. Windsor's."

The receptionist invited the girls to sit down and spoke to the company president on the telephone. When she finished, she said, "Mr. Windsor will see you now. Go down this hall, turn left, and his office is the last room on the right."

The Dana girls had not seen Mr. Windsor for many years, and were not surprised when he said, "I would not have recognized you if I had not been given your names. How are you young ladies? I hear you're amateur sleuths."

The girls laughed and admitted they had had some luck in solving mysteries.

"That's why we're here now," Jean said. "We have brought you a sample of a strange powder and would like you to analyse it."

Mr. Windsor said he would be glad to, then asked where they had obtained the material.

Louise replied, "From a hidden passageway under the mountain peak. By the way, we'd like to keep this a secret."

The company president looked surprised. He asked for more information and Louise told him about their search under Mr. Hodge's home. The chemist was intrigued and said he would analyse the mysterious powder himself.

"You girls stay here. If my phone rings, would you please tell the receptionist that I'll be back in a short time?"

While Louise and Jean were waiting, they looked around the office. There were several cabinets containing specimens of unusual rocks.

They read the labels, and Jean remarked, "This is a good way to get a free education in geology."

Twenty minutes later Mr. Windsor reappeared. He closed the door and said, "You have made quite a find. You'd never guess what that powder is. It's volcanic ash!"

"Volcanic ash?" Louise repeated. "You mean at some time a volcano erupted on the mountain?"

"That's right," Mr. Windsor replied. "It apparently occurred thousands of years ago. Since then, the wind, rain, and sun have covered the ash over with soil, so that people today are not aware of what happened."

Louise told the company president they knew that Grandpa Hodge had made a great discovery. "Do you think this could be it?"

"If it is," Mr. Windsor said, "I wonder why he didn't give the news to the world."

The Danas shrugged, Louise told him that they had found other clues indicating that there was more to the elderly man's secret than just the powder.

Mr. Windsor said he would like to visit the mountain-peak house and see the volcanic ash himself. "I'll try to find the time and meanwhile I'll keep your discovery confidential."

"Thank you," Jean said. "And when you come, bring a surgical mask with you. We sneezed, coughed, and cried a lot down in that passageway."

The man laughed. "I'll do as you say."

Just then his phone buzzed and he picked up the receiver. After listening a couple of moments, he turned to the girls and said, "I have an important long-distance call. Thank you for coming. If you don't mind, I'll keep the sample you brought. I'd like to do a little more testing."

Louise and Jean stood up, waved good-bye, and left. As they drove off, Louise said, "I can't wait to get back and dig some more."

Jean laughed. "First we'd better stop at a chemists and buy surgical masks so we won't sneeze our heads off again."

When they reached a chemists, Jean hopped out of the car and went inside. She purchased a box of disposable surgical masks.

"Now several people can go in the basement at

once to check out that strange tunnel," she told Louise.

As soon as they reached the mountain-peak home, the girls reported Mr. Windsor's findings.

"How exciting!" Aunt Harriet exclaimed. "I'm sure Mr. Hodge wrote about this in his manuscript. No doubt the thief read about it. I wonder, though, if he actually saw the volcanic ash."

"He couldn't have," Tammi spoke up. "I know that stairway has been there for a long time, long before the manuscript was stolen."

Louise and Jean unpacked their surgical masks. "Ready to investigate?" Jean asked Tammi.

"Sure thing. But first, Aunt Harriet and I have a surprise for you."

"Great," Jean said. "What is it?"

"While you were gone, we decided to search for Grandpa's duplicate manuscript. We looked between the pages of every single book in the house," Tammi said. "Many of them contained scribbled notes on separate pieces of paper, but Aunt Harriet and I figured out that they referred to the contents of the books and were comments on certain passages."

"You mean, they had nothing to do with our mystery," Jean said, disappointed.

Tammi grinned and the Dana girls realized that a more dramatic announcement was in store for them.

"Don't keep us in suspense," Louise pleaded.

"I'm sure you have something really important to tell us."

"We do," their aunt replied. "We found two pieces of paper with notations that had nothing to do with the books in which they had been hidden. One of them said, 'What became of the Puma people?' "

"What did the other paper say?" Jean asked.

Tammi replied, "Were the artifacts stolen?"

The Danas were amazed at the revelations. They were positive now that Grandpa Hodge's discovery had something to do with the volcano and with what might have been buried under it as well!

CHAPTER XI

A Sleeping Volcano

"THIS was the second time Grandpa referred to the Puma people," Tammi said thoughtfully. "I wish we knew what he meant by that."

"I'm sure Grandpa Hodge's duplicate manuscript would answer every one of our questions," Jean said.

"I just thought of something," Tammi spoke up. "Maybe some time between Grandpa's death and my coming to see you, the person who stole the original took the copy, too!"

"That's possible," Louise said.

There was silence for a full minute while everyone thought this over. Then Aunt Harriet said, "If the thief has both the original and the duplicate, why is he bothering us?"

Jean suggested, "Perhaps the manuscript described a mystery right in this house, or at least on this mountain peak, and the thief wants to get rid of us so he can investigate the place."

Louise said, "I'm convinced that something important is hidden under the volcanic ash. Why don't we go back to the passageway and dig?"

The girls were eager to start, and Aunt Harriet offered to act as guard on the first floor. When Louise, Jean, and Tammi reached the mysterious tunnel, they all donned surgical masks.

"Where do you think we should begin?" Tammi asked.

The question stumped the Danas. During their previous walk through the passageway, they had not seen any particular spot that looked promising.

"But we can't excavate this whole tunnel!" Tammi said. "What are we going to do?"

Louise pointed out that there was no sense in starting very far from the entrance. "We may have to carry some of this stuff out of here, so the shorter the distance, the better."

"Right," Jean said, and with a flourish stuck her shovel into the ash. She worked furiously for a couple of minutes, then heaved a sigh. The dust fell back into the hole as fast as she scooped it up! "This is a problem," she said. "How are we ever going to clear this out?"

Louise and Tammi, who had not started yet, laughed. Louise said, "Oh, we'll just stand here and watch you work."

Jean made a face at her sister and continued digging. This time she threw the shovelful of ash a greater distance, so it could not run back into the hole.

Tammi asked, "Aren't we going to use the pails to carry out the ash? We could pile it up in one of the sheds."

"Good idea," Louise said, and started to dig.

The girls worked for nearly an hour, lugging out bucket after bucket. When they had made a good-sized hole, Tammi's shovel hit something hard. Carefully she reached down and lifted up a solid object.

"I wonder what it is?" she said, brushing it off.

"Let me see," Louise said. She played her flashlight on the find, which proved to be a carved figurine.

"It looks like an animal," Tammi said. "Do you think——"

"Yes," Louise interrupted. "It's a puma!"

"A puma!" Jean cried out. "It must have belonged to the Puma people that Mr. Hodge wrote about!"

The three girls stared at one another, puzzling thoughts racing through their minds.

Louise said, "What I can't understand is what your Grandpa Hodge meant by 'Puma people.' Did he refer to the cats themselves, or to a tribe of people who held the puma sacred?"

Jean suggested that they take the carving upstairs and show it to Aunt Harriet. "Besides, we can examine it under a stronger light."

When Miss Dana saw the puma statuette, she was amazed. After looking at it closely, she said, "Remember the second notation we found? It said something about stolen artifacts. I wonder if Grandpa Hodge meant this kind of artifact?"

"What I'd like to know," Jean put in, "is whether he hid this statuette or never even knew it was there?"

Louise washed the stone so that the markings would be more distinct. Then she held it under a bright lamp. The puma had been carefully carved by a sculptor with great talent.

"This settles one thing," Louise remarked. "No primitive could have done this. I'm sure that the 'Puma people' Mr. Hodge referred to belonged to some ancient civilisation."

"And you think they were buried under the volcano?" Tammi asked.

Louise nodded. "The question is, how far down do we have to dig to find more evidence?"

Jean laughed. "At the rate we're going, it'll take us the rest of our lives to go even another ten feet!"

Miss Dana suggested that while the girls were trying to figure out what to do, she would show them a discovery of her own. She pointed to a table she had pulled away from the wall. To everyone's surprise, there was a low cupboard behind it, which they had not noticed before.

"A lot of books are in there," Aunt Harriet said. "I've checked through the pages, but found nothing handwritten. The books are on archeological subjects and several of them are on American Indians."

Tammi told the Danas that her grandfather had often told her about American Indians in ancient times.

"Were any of them about volcanos?" Jean asked.

"No," Tammi replied. "Not pumas, either. But there were a lot of good tales about Mexican jaguars and serpents, and the customs of the people who lived in South America at that time."

"Why don't you tell us one of them?" Aunt Harriet suggested. "We might even pick up a clue to our mystery."

Louise and Jean liked the idea, and Tammi began one of her grandfather's stories. "Long, long ago, around one thousand A.D., the Incas lived in South America. They controlled a tremendous amount of territory. In those days it was difficult to get messages from one place to another."

Tammi smiled. "That sounds funny now, doesn't it, with telephones, telegraph, cars, and airplanes?"

The others agreed, and she went on, "The Incas were a highly civilised people and were great builders. They mined tons and tons of gold and the wealthy lords of the empire used it to decorate their headdresses and robes.

"One of the most amazing things they created was a way to get messages from one place to another very fast. Men called *chasqui* were trained from early childhood to run at tremendous speed in the high altitudes. They could cover a mile in six and a half minutes."

"Wow!" Jean exclaimed. "They must have had enormous lung expansion."

"They did," Tammi said. "The Incas built very wide, smooth roads to make it easy for these runners to speed despite traffic. Each man had to run only one mile and a half at a time, then another courier continued the journey. This way, no one became exhausted.

"Along the roads were huts called *o'kla*, where the messengers stopped to rest. According to history, there were always a couple of guards at these posts.

"The Incas had no form of writing, so all the messages were given by word of mouth from one *chasqui* to another. Much of this information was of a highly secret nature, and there was a death penalty for any *chasqui* found giving away the secret except to the next *chasqui*."

When Tammi stopped speaking, Jean said, "That was something like our relay games. Only the stick one runner hands to another doesn't hold a secret!"

Suddenly Homer started to bark furiously. Tammi and the Danas rushed to the front window and looked out. They saw no one, but an instant later they heard the sound of a rifle shot!

CHAPTER XII

Forced Entry

AT THE crack of the shot Louise and Jean froze in fright. They stared out the window and for a few seconds no one spoke.

Finally Louise broke the silence. "Do—do you think there are hunters around here?"

"I don't believe they'd come that close to the house," Tammi said. "Besides, this is private property."

"We should go and see if Homer's all right," Jean said.

"No!" Aunt Harriet cried out emphatically. "If someone's out there with a gun, you might be hit!"

"What are we going to do?" Jean asked.

"Let's look out all the windows, but make sure we're not being seen," Louise suggested. "Perhaps we can determine who's there."

Each of them went from window to window, glancing in all directions. Nothing moved outside, and there was no one in sight.

"I can't even find Homer," Louise said, worried. "I hope he wasn't hit!"

"Suppose we open the door just a bit and call him?" Jean suggested.

"All right," Aunt Harriet agreed. "But make sure you're not a target."

The girls went to the front door and opened it a crack. "Homer! Homer!" Louise called.

"I'll yell out the rear window," Jean offered. "He might not hear if he's in the back."

Their strategy was successful. A few minutes later Louise noticed Homer slinking toward her. He appeared to be frightened.

"Homer!" she exclaimed in relief. "Come in, quick!"

She opened the door momentarily, stepping behind it. The animal entered the house and the next moment she banged the door shut.

"Jean, come here!" Louise called out. "Homer is all right!"

The Danas patted the German shepherd, relieved and grateful that he was not hurt.

"Do you think the shot missed him?" Jean asked. She examined the dog.

"I have a hunch it was only meant to frighten us," Louise commented. "After all, if someone wanted to shoot Homer and missed, why didn't he try again?"

Aunt Harriet nodded. "It is rather odd that only one bullet was fired. Let's wait a while, then go outside and see if we can find a clue to the rifleman."

An hour later Aunt Harriet felt it was safe to venture outdoors. She and the girls looked all around. After searching thoroughly for footprints and other clues, Jean called out, "Look! There's a bullet hole in the side of the house!"

"I think we should call the police," Louise said. "This proves beyond a doubt that the rifleman was not a hunter."

"Mr. Fife will be here in a short while," Aunt Harriet said. "Let's tell him what happened and let him decide what to do about it."

When the detective arrived and heard the story, he was disturbed. "We need more protection on this mountain," he said. "I'll phone headquarters and ask for increased patrol of the property."

As soon as he had done this and his request was granted, the Danas and Tammi decided to leave. Telling Mr. Fife that they hoped he would have no trouble during the night, they drove off.

The next morning, when the group returned to the Hodge home, Mr. Fife reported that there had been no disturbance. "Homer did not bark once. He slept soundly, and so did I."

After the detective had left, the girls tidied the house a bit. This reminded Aunt Harriet to call Cora Appel at the Dana home to tell her what chores to take care of that day. She dialled the number but there was no answer. Miss Dana assumed that Cora had not yet arrived.

"That's strange," she said. "Cora is very reliable and prompt. If she didn't plan to come, she would have phoned."

Fifteen minutes later Aunt Harriet called again. After a long wait, she heard the receiver fall to the floor, but no one picked it up or spoke. Aunt Harriet wondered if there was a stranger in the house.

"Cora, are you there?" she asked.

Finally there was a muffled reply. "I'm—a prisoner. I'm—tied up!"

Aunt Harriet was shocked. "We'll rescue you," she said. "Keep up your courage!" She put down the phone and told the girls what Cora had said, then declared she was going home at once to take care of the matter.

"Let me come with you," Louise offered.

Aunt Harriet shook her head. "No. I think you should stay here, guard this place, and go on with your investigation. I'll phone our next door neighbour. She has a key, you know. I'll ask her to contact the police and they can all go in at once."

After placing the call, Aunt Harriet drove off,

leaving the girls wondering what had happened at the Dana home. Had a burglar been there to rob the place, or was the incident connected with the mystery they were working on?

"What are we going to do next?" Jean asked.

"Suppose we go back to the cellar and dig some more in the volcanic ash," Louise suggested.

Tammi asked, "Why don't I stay up here with Homer and watch for visitors or intruders? I'd like to get more clothes and a few other things from my room anyway. You girls go ahead."

The Danas hesitated. "I don't think you should be up here alone," Jean said finally. "Too many dangerous things have happened. We'll forget the digging for a while and stay with you."

"All right," Tammi agreed. "Let's get my things first, and later we'll investigate the cellar."

When the girls reached Tammi's room, she opened a drawer and took out a couple of sweaters. Then she laid out several skirts. In the meantime, Louise and Jean were glancing around the room. It was full of pictures, most of which, Tammi said, were of her school friends.

"But that's a photo of Grandpa Hodge on the dressing table," she added. "Isn't he wonderful?"

Louise and Jean looked at the elderly man. "What a kindly expression he has!" Jean said. "And he's so handsome. Tammi, you resemble him a good bit."

"That's what people tell me," the girl replied. "Look at the message on the back."

Louise turned the photograph over. There was nothing on it!

Tammi said, "Lift the picture out."

Louise did, and read, "To my lovely Tammi, a marvellous companion. Grandpa Hodge."

"That's sweet," Louise said as she tucked the photograph back into the frame. "He must have been very proud of you."

"I guess so," Tammi replied. "Anyway, he taught me so many things. I'll always try to live up to his expectations."

The phone rang. "Maybe that's Aunt Harriet," Louise said and hurried into the late Mr. Hodge's bedroom to answer it. Jean and Tammi followed.

The caller was indeed Aunt Harriet. She said that by the time she had reached home, the neighbour and the police had already arrived and untied Cora, who was hysterical.

"She told me she was working in the kitchen when two men opened the front door with a key and came in. They began to ransack the house. Cora went to see what was going on, and they grabbed her. They tied a gag across her mouth and bound her hands and ankles.

"Poor Cora couldn't move, and had to watch as the men, who wore masks, looked through every drawer and the desk in the living room. They seemed angry because they couldn't find what they were hunting for. Finally they left."

"Then what happened?" Louise asked.

"Cora tried to loosen her bonds, but failed. She attempted to remove the gag by rubbing the back of her head against a table leg. She managed to shift it enough so that when the phone rang, she could at least knock the receiver off its cradle and mumble about her predicament."

"Did Cora give the police a description of the men?" Louise asked.

"She couldn't because of the masks. She also said they wore gloves and left no fingerprints."

"Did they take anything from the house?"

"No," her aunt answered. "I wonder what they were looking for."

"Maybe they thought we took the duplicate manuscript home for safekeeping," Louise said.

"Either that or they figured we found something else and brought it over here," Aunt Harriet added. "Perhaps they read in the original that Mr. Hodge had discovered ancient artifacts. They might have searched the Hodge house in vain for them and decided to check ours next."

Louise sighed. "There are so many possibilities. All we can do is guess. What are you going to do next, Aunt Harriet?"

"I'll stay home today and straighten out the mess these fellows left," Miss Dana said. "But first

I'll drive Cora home. She's still pretty upset, even though she has calmed down a lot since I arrived. But I think she'll feel better if I give her the day off."

"Okay," Louise said. "Suppose we call you when Mr. Fife comes and then you can pick us up?"

"Good idea. Meanwhile, I hope there won't be any more trouble. Good-bye for now."

"What did your aunt say?" Tammi asked.

Jean added, "We tried to listen but couldn't hear very well."

Both girls were shocked when they learned the news, and Tammi looked worried.

"Oh dear," she said with a sigh. "I had no idea I would get you in such danger when I asked you to help me with the mystery. I'm terribly sorry."

"It's not your fault," Louise said. "Besides, the intruders didn't take anything from the house, so no great harm has been done. Please don't worry any more."

"All right," Tammi replied. "I do feel sad about poor Cora, though. I'm sure she was scared silly by those horrible men."

"No doubt," Louise agreed. "We'll have to think of something nice for her to make up for what happened. But before we do anything else, how about some lunch? I'm starving."

"So am I," Jean said with a laugh.

The girls made sandwiches and Tammi got some fresh fruit from the pantry. While they ate, the three discussed how they would spend the afternoon.

"I think we should—" Jean started to say, then stopped suddenly. Homer was barking wildly!

The girls jumped up and ran to the window. They saw a car being driven up the hill. A look of fear came over Tammi's face.

"Who can that be?" she asked apprehensively.

CHAPTER XIII

Unexpected Drop

THE car stopped in front of the house and three young men stepped out.

"It's Ken, Chris, and another boy," Louise exclaimed in relief when she recognized their friends. She opened the door and Jean followed her to greet the callers, while Tammi stood shyly in the doorway.

"How great to see you!" Louise said to Ken Scott, who kissed her while Jean hugged her favourite date, Chris Barton.

Ken grinned. "When I received your letter, Louise, I thought we might be able to help you with the mystery. And we brought Paul Burke, who is a neighbour of ours."

"Hello, Paul," Louise said and shook hands with the good-looking fourteen-year-old.

After introductions, Tammi asked the young people to come inside. Everyone followed her into the living room, and Jean said, "Louise, I didn't know you wrote to Ken. When did you find the time? Things have been so hectic around here."

Ken grinned. "You know I'm such a wonderful guy that she can't help but find the time."

Louise laughed. "Talk about a big head!"

"Who, me?" Ken quipped.

"You can prove how great you are by helping us solve this mystery," Louise told him. "That's why I wrote. We could use some assistance."

Ken hung his head in mock despair. "I should have known it wasn't because of me. It was because you wanted something!"

When the teasing stopped, Chris said, "Now tell us all about your new case. If strong arms are required, we've got six of them. Will that do?"

"That'll be fine," Jean said. "We could also use the heads that come with the muscle. Perhaps one of you can figure out how volcanic ash got into Tammi's basement."

"Volcanic ash?" Chris was puzzled.

"Right," Jean replied, and explained what they had discovered. Both Chris and Ken were intrigued and said they could not wait to start investigating.

Paul, meanwhile, had sat down next to Tammi and told her that he, too, owned a German shepherd. He saw Mr. Fife's dog when they pulled up in front of the house. Tammi told him how well-trained Homer was. Soon the two got up and walked outside to play with the dog.

Louise smiled. "I guess they don't want to come with us," she said. "It's just as well. They can guard the house while Jean and I introduce you boys to the volcanic mystery."

She went to get surgical masks for everyone, then called to Tammi that they were going downstairs. "Please watch the house and answer the phone," she said.

"Okay," Tammi replied.

When the Danas and their friends reached the passageway, Ken and Chris were amazed to see the gray-white powder. They started to enlarge the hole. Since the boys were able to throw the ash a greater distance than the girls, they decided not to use the buckets.

Soon the hole became deeper. The sides were almost like quicksand, however, and from time to time large portions spilled into the excavation.

"At this rate we'll never finish," Ken remarked.

Chris said practically, "There has to be solid ground underneath this ash, or we would sink. Let's just dig a little more."

It was not long before his shovel hit a firm surface. "I think I've found it," Chris called out.

Jean jumped into the pit and tried to penetrate the bottom with her shovel. Suddenly it gave way, and she felt herself sinking. The next second both she and Chris tumbled headlong into a dark hole!

Louise and Ken cried out in horror. "Jean! Chris! Are you all right?"

The only reply was a muffled cough. Ken and Louise could hardly see through the heavy cloud of ash that had been stirred up, and they had to close their eyes momentarily.

When the dust settled somewhat, Ken called again, and this time Chris answered. "We're all right. Drop a flashlight down. And get us out of here before we sneeze to death."

"What happened to your masks?" Louise asked.

"They were knocked off when we fell. I found them, but they're all dusty."

Ken turned to Louise. "Is there any rope in the house?"

"I'll run upstairs and ask Tammi."

"Okay. And see if you can find a long, strong board."

Louise dashed off. She realized that Ken planned to lay the board across the hole after tying one end of the rope around it. She called Tammi and Paul and met them in the hallway and quickly told them what had happened.

"Oh dear," Tammi cried out in alarm. "I hope Chris and Jean weren't hurt!"

"I think they're okay," Louise assured her. "Have you some rope or a clothesline at hand, and also a long board?"

Tammi nodded. "Yes, in the garage."

The three quickly gathered the needed items and returned to the passageway. Ken placed the board across the opening, then stepped on it, and tied one end of the rope securely around the centre. Then he let the other one down into the hole.

"Grab it and try to climb up," he advised. "We'll help pull you out as soon as we can get hold of you."

He turned to Louise and Tammi. "You stand on each end of the board so it doesn't shift. I'll stay in the middle and help Chris and Jean."

"Okay," Louise said and the two positioned themselves.

"I'm coming up first," Chris announced. "Jean insisted because she has the flashlight and is checking this place out. Also, we figure if the rope holds me, she won't have any problem because she's lighter."

"All right," Ken said.

Chris took the rope and started to climb. He had no trouble and knew Jean would not have any either, since all the young people were good athletes. Soon his head appeared. Ken reached down and grabbed his friend under the arms. A second later Chris was free.

"Boy, am I glad to be out of that hole!" he exclaimed, his face covered with ash. He sneezed. "We'd better get Jean now."

Ken called down to the girl. There was no answer. Louise's heart sank. What had happened to her sister?

Ken repeated his call. There was a faint reply, then Jean's voice came stronger. "This might have been another tunnel running underneath the passageway. But it has caved in on both sides."

"How large an area is it?" Louise asked.

"Oh, only about seven feet wide and maybe ten feet long. The floor is covered with ash, too, and there seems to be nothing down here. I've been poking around—wait a minute!"

"What is it?" Tammi asked. "Did you find something?"

"I sure did. It's another artifact!" Jean exclaimed, elated. "I'll tie the rope around it. You haul it up first, because I can't hold onto it while I climb."

The others waited until Jean said she was ready. Then Ken pulled up the rope. Attached to it was a copper statue of a warrior!

Ken unfastened it and handed it to Louise. "What a marvellous find," she remarked. "But before we examinc it any closer, let's rescue Jean."

Ken let the rope down again. Jean grabbed it and pulled herself up.

What a sight she was! Her hair was white and she sneezed continuously. But she was safe!

Louise declared that they should quit work for the day, and led the way out of the passage up to the first floor. Jean went to Tammi's room, and Chris to Grandpa Hodge's.

Tammi found the nasal and throat sprays Aunt Harriet had used, and soon the medication relieved the victims' symptoms.

After baths and shampoos, the two young people felt fine again. The group gathered in the living room and talked about their discovery. They had cleaned the warrior with copper polish. On the bottom was the distinct footprint of a puma.

"The Puma people again," Tammi said. "Oh, when are we going to learn their secret?"

"I have a strong hunch," Louise remarked, "that we are near a solution."

"I hope you're right," said Jean. "I must tell you what I think about this area." She said that after finding the warrior, she had felt around the sides of the hole into which she had tumbled.

"There was a little niche where the floor and walls were made of stone blocks. It probably wasn't a tunnel, after all, but a building of some kind may have stood there in ancient times, maybe a tower."

"But why was a passageway above it?" Louise asked.

"Who knows? It may have been constructed much later."

"But both the building beneath and the passageway contained volcanic ash," Ken observed.

"True. Perhaps the tunnel was originally part of the tower, a lookout, for instance. Later someone could have enlarged it."

Louise sighed. "We'll probably never know. And now I think I'd better call Aunt Harriet and tell her she doesn't have to pick us up."

She went to the telephone and told her aunt about the boys' arrival, and their adventure in the tunnel. "You won't have to come and get us," she added. "The boys have a car. But we'll be ready for one of your great dinners!"

After the phone call, Tammi said, "Paul and I made a discovery, too!"

"What is it?" Louise asked.

"Well," Tammi replied, "we wanted to do some detecting, so we went into Grandpa Hodge's den. This time Paul rolled up the rug to examine the floor. And what do you think we found?"

"What?" the others chorussed.

"Come along and we'll show you!"

They got up from the table. Just then Homer started to bark.

"Oh, dear, more trouble," Tammi said, and ran to the window. "I don't see anyone!" she reported.

"We'll go out and check," Chris offered, and the boys went into the yard.

Homer had disappeared to the back of the house, and the three followed. Presently they returned to the kitchen.

"What was it?" Jean asked.

Paul grinned. "We didn't see any intruders, but we noticed a rabbit running for dear life!"

The girls' laughter broke the tension. "Good old

Homer," Tammi said. "At least he's having some fun, too!"

Then she and Paul led the way to the den. The carpet was still rolled back, and in the centre of the floor was a metal ring.

"We got only this far when you came up from the basement for the rope and the board," Paul explained. "What do you think is under there?"

"Open it and let's find out!" Jean urged.

CHAPTER XIV

A Valuable Clue

THE floorboard with the ring in Grandpa Hodge's den was loose. Ken pulled it up easily.

"Look at this!" Tammi exclaimed. She reached down and lifted out an artist's portfolio. She laid it on the desk and turned back the cover. On the first page was a fine drawing of a puma.

"Another clue!" Jean exclaimed. "Let's see what the rest of the pictures are."

All the sketches were pencil drawings. Some depicted wild cats, others volcanos in various stages of eruption. Several represented prehistoric Indian villages with caves, simple stone dwellings, and mud huts. Each drawing had a question mark on it, but no words. None were signed.

"Do you think Grandpa made these?" Tammi asked.

"Most likely," Louise replied. "Evidently these are representations of what he thought the volcano and the ancient Indian villages looked like. But why?"

"Perhaps Mr. Hodge wanted to use the sketches as illustrations in his manuscript," Chris suggested. "Did he ever mention this to you, Tammi?"

"No. I've already told Louise and Jean that I didn't even know the manuscript existed until the day he died."

"Too bad there aren't any notes in this portfolio," Chris said. He grinned. "You Danas have really picked out a beauty this time. If we're going to help you solve this mystery before we go home, we'll have to hurry."

Louise laughed. "That reminds me. We didn't even ask how long you're staying."

"We'll have to be back by tomorrow night."

"What do you suggest we do now?" Louise asked.

"First, let's return the portfolio to its hiding place," Jean said. "Obviously our enemies don't know about it, or they would have stolen it. Now the house is so well guarded that nobody is taking anything away."

The young people put the portfolio back under the floorboard and rolled the rug in place. They spent the rest of the afternoon searching the dining room, but found no clues. When Mr. Fife arrived, the girls introduced Ken, Chris, and Paul, then the group said good night and drove to the Dana home.

Aunt Harriet greeted the boys affectionately,

and as promised, had a sumptuous dinner for them. While they were eating, Jean said, "How would you all like to go to a dance tonight?"

"Sounds great," Chris replied. "Where is it?"

Jean explained that the affair was being held at the local women's club for the benefit of a technical school for handicapped people.

"Aunt Harriet bought a block of tickets, but until you boys came, we didn't expect to use them," she said.

The young people were enthusiastic about going. They changed their clothes, then said good-bye to Aunt Harriet.

The club's large auditorium was already filled with people. Tables had been arranged around the sides of the room, with the centre left for dancing, and a band was playing on the stage.

The Danas and their friends selected a table for six and sat down. They ordered tall glasses of iced orange juice, then all of them got up to dance.

A slow number followed a fast one and Ken put his arms around Louise as he led her expertly across the hardwood floor. Suddenly he felt her stiffen.

"What's the matter?" he asked. "Is something bothering you?"

"I just saw a man over there," Louise whispered. "He looked like Zavier Roundtree!"

"What?"

"Yes! He's sitting at a table we just passed."

"He'd be the last person I would expect to be at this dance," Ken said thoughtfully.

"I feel the same way. Perhaps I'd better go back and make sure it's really Zavier Roundtree before I call the police."

"I'll go with you," Ken offered. "Shall we just dance by, or do you want to approach him from another direction?"

"He was facing the band," Louise said. "If he sees me approach on the dance floor, he will probably take off before we get there. Why don't we walk up from behind?"

"Good idea," Ken said, and both stopped dancing. They wound their way past several tables and went toward the man Louise had seen. When they reached the spot, she stopped short.

"Ken!" she whispered. "I must have made a mistake! This man is handicapped. He's sitting in a wheelchair!"

"He could be faking," Ken said. "Why don't you talk to him?"

"I will," Louise said and walked up to the stranger. "Excuse me," she said, "but you look like someone I've met. Would you mind telling me your name?"

"I don't mind a bit," the man replied pleasantly. "It's Roundtree, Ralph Roundtree."

Louise was thunderstruck. "Do you have a brother named Zavier?"

"He's my twin," the man replied. "It's strange

you should ask. I haven't seen him in many years, and no one in the family has any idea where he is. Do you know where he lives?"

"No, but I've seen him in Oak Falls recently."

"Is he a friend of yours?"

"N-no. But I'd like to get in touch with him and ask him a few questions. What's the last address you have for him?"

"All I know is that he lived in Sayreville," Ralph Roundtree replied. "And that was quite a while ago. How did you meet my brother?"

"Oh, I just ran into him in the street," Louise said evasively. "I'll try to get in touch with him in Sayreville. And thank you very much."

Before the man had a chance to ask further questions, she wished him a pleasant evening and, followed by Ken, went back to their table.

The music had stopped and their four companions were already seated.

"I just picked up a clue," Louise announced, and told the group what she had learned.

Jean was excited by the information and suggested that they go to Sayreville the next day to investigate.

"But somebody has to guard my home," Tammi reminded her. "How would it be if Aunt Harriet, Paul, and I go there, and the rest of you drive to Savreville?"

The Danas thought this arrangement was excellent and later, when they told Aunt Harriet of the plan, she agreed.

The following morning the two groups set off. Ken had looked up Sayreville on the map and had no trouble finding his way.

"Where do you want to start your hunt?" he asked as they drove along the main street.

Louise pointed to a telephone booth. "Why don't you stop over there so we can check if Zavier Roundtree is listed in the directory?"

Ken parked and she hopped out. Louise looked under Sayreville and all the surrounding towns, but Roundtree's name did not appear. Disappointed, she returned to the car.

Jean suggested that they go to police headquarters and ask if the man was known. The sergeant on duty replied, "Roundtree? Sounds familiar. Let me see if he's on our wanted list." He consulted a large register on his desk. "No, I can't find him. I must have heard his name in some other connection."

Louise thanked the officer and the young people returned to the car.

"Does anyone have a suggestion on where to try next?" Jean asked.

Chris said, "How about garages and petrol stations?"

The Danas liked the idea and began a systematic tour through town. No one had heard of Zavier

Roundtree, and the young people had almost given up hope when they came to Howie's Service and Repair Shop. Ken pulled up to the fuel pump.

"I'll get petrol while we're here," he said. "Louise and Jean, suppose you question the owner."

The girls got out of the car and walked into the office. The gray-haired proprietor was seated at a desk, writing bills.

"Pardon me," Louise said. "We're trying to locate a man named Zavier Roundtree. Is he by any chance a customer of yours?"

Howie looked up. "It's funny you should ask. He was here only a few days ago, getting his car fixed. Said he had a slight accident. Went in and out of a pothole too fast."

Jean asked if Howie knew where Roundtree lived.

"No, I'm sorry." The man looked quizzically at the girls. "Is he a friend of yours? He doesn't exactly seem to be your kind of folk."

"He's not a friend," Jean said. "But we'd like to get in touch with him."

The garage owner said he did know one thing that might help the girls. "I have his licence number." He wrote it on a piece of paper.

"Thank you very much," Louise said. Then the Danas said good-bye to the friendly proprietor and left. They jumped into the car and waited for Ken to drive off before telling their friends what they had learned.

"We picked up a marvellous clue," Louise said. "Howie gave us Zavier Roundtree's licence number. It's not the same, though, as the one on the green sedan he drove when he followed us from the mountain peak."

"He must have been using someone else's car that time," Chris suggested.

As they approached a wayside telephone, Louise said she wanted to alert the Oak Falls police. Ken stopped and she made the call.

Chief Ignari thanked her and said he would send out an alarm at once to have the car stopped and the driver picked up.

The young people left Sayreville and arrived at home before Aunt Harriet, Tammi, and Paul.

"I suppose we should start dinner," Louise said.

"We'll be glad to help," Ken offered. "You know we're both good cooks!"

"I know," Louise replied. "But how good are you on preparation?"

"Like what?"

"Like peeling potatoes!"

Chris made a face, but both boys said they were game. Jean took them at their word and brought out potatoes, a saucepan, and two knives.

"Enjoy yourselves," she said and walked off.

Dinner was ready when Aunt Harriet, Tammi, and Paul drove up.

"Mmm, smells good," Aunt Harriet said as they walked in the door. "Did you have any luck today?"

"Yes, we did," Louise answered. "No one knew Zavier Roundtree's address, but we got the licence number of his car and reported it to the police. How about you?"

Tammi's eyes were sparkling. "Wait until we tell you what happened at my home today!" she said.

CHAPTER XV

A Treasure Safe

"WHAT?" Louise and Jean asked in unison.

"After you girls drove off with Ken and Chris," Tammi began, "Paul and I decided to see if there were other loose floorboards in the den. We discovered no more rings, but we rocked back and forth on several boards to find out if any of them moved."

"And we discovered one!" Paul took up the story. "Tammi got a screwdriver and we lifted up one end."

"Underneath were a lot of small pieces of paper," Tammi added. "They were in Grandpa's handwriting, but we couldn't make any sense out of them."

"Did you bring the slips along?" Jean asked eagerly.

"We sure did," Tammi replied. "Paul has them."

The boy had stuffed the papers into his jeans pocket. Now he took them out and laid them on the dining-room table.

Jean turned on the bright overhead light, and everyone looked to see what was written on the scraps.

Chris asked Tammi, "Are you positive your grandfather told you nothing about these things?"

The girl shook her head and smiled. "He never discussed his work with me. I guess he thought I couldn't keep a secret! During the summer, when I was home from school, I went to day camp, and when I wasn't practicing the piano at night, Grandpa would play games with me and tell me stories."

Jean read one note after another. "Most of them contain only a word or two," she said. "I wonder if Grandpa Hodge used them as some sort of index."

"Could be," Louise said. "But it's also possible that they're part of a puzzle that makes sense if the fragments are placed in the proper order."

"You mean, we might be able to piece together a message?" Tammi asked.

"Let's try," Ken suggested.

Jean picked one up. "This says *prehistoric volcano*," she said. "Perhaps we can use it as a starting point and arrange the others around it."

The group worked for several minutes in silence,

then Ken said, "I have *ancient pottery*, *round vases*, and *Copper City*. The first two are similar, but where would *Copper City* fit in?"

"Who knows?" Tammi asked. "I don't have anything that would go with *Copper City*."

"Neither do I," Jean said, and the others just shrugged.

"Probably it was at the bottom of the volcano," Tammi said.

Louise moved the piece alongside the one saying *prehistoric volcano*. Again there was silence for a while. Finally Aunt Harriet said, "Does anyone have something referring to this note? It says *Puma superstitions*."

Louise giggled. "Superstitions, sayings, ghosts, apparitions, ESP—"

Everyone searched among their scraps of paper and reported nothing in the above categories, until Chris came up with *river stars*.

Paul grimaced. "Do you mean there were stars in the river, or a river in the stars?"

The others laughed. Tammi said, "Maybe it means a reflection of the stars in the river."

Louise thought this was a good answer. "Perhaps stars shining on the river brought good luck to people," she said.

"I wonder," Tammi remarked, "if Grandpa Hodge knew the answer himself."

Jean reminded her that until they found the

manuscript, no one could answer that question.

Another half hour went by, and the group was no nearer a solution than they had been when they started. Finally Chris said, "This is the hardest jigsaw puzzle I've ever tried to put together!"

Ken looked at his watch. "Chris," he said, "we must leave. We have a long drive and it will be after midnight before we get home."

Tammi spoke. "Do you really have to? Everything is getting to be so interesting." She glanced at Paul, and the look did not escape the notice of her friends.

"Sorry, Tammi, but we must," Ken said. "Chris has to do a job for his father tomorrow, and I have to take my mother to the doctor. But we'll be back as soon as we can."

"You, too?" Tammi asked and glanced at Paul.

"I wouldn't miss the opportunity to do some more sleuthing for anything in the world," Paul replied with a grin. "I really enjoyed myself and I'm so glad I met you!"

Tammi blushed and the boys said good-bye.

After they had left, Tammi decided to go to bed. Aunt Harriet, too, admitted that she had had a long day and wanted to retire.

She smiled at her nieces. "I suppose you'll stay up a while and work on this puzzle."

"You're right," Louise replied.

She and Jean kissed their aunt and Tammi good-night, then turned back to the pieces of paper on the table. They continued to move the various notations from place to place, but nothing seemed to fit.

"Maybe," Louise said, "Copper City was right here on the mountainside."

"And perhaps the volcano ruined not only the city, but the copper industry as well," Jean added.

It was nearly two o'clock by the time the girls decided to quit. They realized that there were great gaps in the story of what might have happened on the mountain peak many centuries ago, and the notes would not provide any further clues.

Jean giggled. "You know that passageway might have been a road in Copper City. Quantities of ash may have sifted in before the ends were closed up. It's just possible we were walking down Main Street, Copper City, Postal Code 00000."

Louise laughed. "I think Main Street was underneath the tunnel, and the passageway was called Ash Avenue."

Jean declared that they were both getting silly and had better go to bed. She turned off the light, and the sisters climbed the stairs to their room.

The following morning Aunt Harriet and the three girls set off for the mountain-peak home. All were eager to see if there were more valuable clues hidden under the floorboards. As before, they rocked back and forth on the wide strips to see if any others were loose.

Suddenly Louise called out, "Hold it!"

"Did you find one?" Jean asked.

"No. But it's Tammi's house and I think she should be the one to make the next discovery."

The Danas moved to the side of the room, and Tammi went from one floorboard to another. The onlooker's had just about given up the idea, when she stopped.

"I think this one's loose!" she exclaimed.

The Danas came closer. No doubt about it, the board was moving slightly!

Jean told Tammi to step on one end, but her weight was not enough to lift the other one sufficiently. Aunt Harriet walked up beside her. Now the opposite end of the board rose about half an inch.

Jean hurried to get the screwdriver Tammi had used the day before, and the board was quickly prized up.

"Look!" Tammi cried out. "Isn't that a safe?"

"It sure is," Jean replied. She kneeled on the floor to examine the small box, which lay face up, showing a circle of numbers around a handle. She tried the handle, but it did not budge.

"It's locked tight," she remarked.

Louise said they would never get it open unless they learned the combination for dialling the numbers. Tammi and the Danas felt frustrated. They wondered if the missing manuscript was inside.

Aunt Harriet suggested that they phone Mr. Hunter. Louise called him and asked his advice.

The executor was interested. "I'll come right over," he said, "and have a safe expert meet me at your house."

Mr. Hunter arrived first and studied the safe, which was still lying on the floor. He lifted it up and examined it closely, but found no clue to the combination.

The dog barked and another car drove up. Mr. Hunter went outside and brought in a stout, short man of forty, whom he introduced as Jim Jolly. Jolly shook hands with everyone, then said he would like to start work.

When he glanced at the little safe, he smiled and said, "I'll have this open for you in a jiffy."

Louise and Jean looked at each other. It could not be too soon for them!

As the group watched, Jim Jolly put his ear to the safe and turned the dials, first to the left, then to the right. He picked out different numbers and apparently heard a series of slight clicks. Finally he turned the handle, but the door did not budge!

The safe expert frowned. "I can't understand it," he said. "It should open!"

He continued to turn the dial and try the handle over and over. At last he had success. As he moved the knob, the door lifted up!

Mr. Hunter stepped forward. "Thank you," he said. "That'll be all."

A look of disappointment came over Jim Jolly's face. Evidently he was curious to see what was in the safe, but Mr. Hunter did not intend to let him find out.

He paid the expert and escorted him to the door. After Jim Jolly had driven off and Mr. Hunter locked the front door, he returned to the safe. Tammi and the Danas had politely waited for him, although their curiosity was almost getting the better of them.

He opened the small door. Inside the box lay not the missing manuscript, but several ancient artifacts, together with a list.

"Grandpa must have found these!" Tammi exclaimed. "Aren't they wonderful!"

Everything was made of copper—knives, a helmet, part of a bowl, something the girls guessed was a chain sash, and a matching bracelet and anklet.

"I wonder where Mr. Hodge located these," Louise spoke up. "Do you suppose they were in the ash?"

No one had an answer. The artifacts could have been anywhere in the buried city.

"They must be very valuable," Aunt Harriet suggested. She studied the list and said, "The helmet is described under number twenty-five. The bracelet, sash, and anklet are twenty-six. The bowl is item twenty-seven, and the knives are twenty-eight."

Jean looked over her shoulder. "This means

Grandpa Hodge found twenty-four additional artifacts." She read all the descriptions. When she finished, Jean said, "The pieces we discovered under the ash and in the pit aren't on this list!"

Aunt Harriet frowned. "This suggests that Mr. Hodge did not hide those pieces and perhaps didn't know they existed."

"And where are the twenty-four missing artifacts?" Tammi asked.

"Perhaps he sold them," Jean said.

"I doubt that," Louise objected. "Since he kept his discoveries a secret, I think he would have held on to them until he was ready to release all his information."

Mr. Hunter agreed. "I have a hunch that the missing objects are in this house somewhere," he said. "I hope you girls will unearth them. Meanwhile, I'll put these in the bank vault, as part of John Hodge's estate."

"May we keep the list?" Jean asked. "We can compare it with anything else we may discover."

"Of course," Mr. Hunter said.

He and the girls carefully wrapped the articles and put them into a bag. Then they returned the safe to its hiding place under the floorboard.

Aunt Harriet said, "Mr. Hodge did an excellent polishing job on the artifacts. They are certainly clean and shiny."

Mr. Hunter looked into space for a few seconds,

then said, "What you say is true, Miss Dana. It's just possible that Mr. Hodge didn't dig them up."

"What do you mean?" Tammi asked.

"He could have purchased them," Mr. Hunter replied.

Tammi's eyes blazed, and she grew red in the face. "My grandfather told me he made a great discovery, and I believe he spoke the truth!"

CHAPTER XVI

Puzzling Phone Call

MR. HUNTER put an arm around Tammi's shoulders. "No one doubts your grandfather's honesty. But he never said he found these artifacts, did he? He could have bought them as an investment, or just for his own enjoyment, and they might have nothing to do with his discovery."

Louise spoke up. "I'm sure the ancient objects were not purchased. They look too much like the others we found—the material is the same, and the style is similar."

Mr. Hunter nodded. "I agree with you. It's just that I thought we should consider all the possibilities."

Tammi calmed down and the girls escorted Mr. Hunter out to his car. After he had left, they returned to the house. The telephone rang.

"Who is calling?" Louise asked.

A woman answered in a clipped tone. "I'll tell Tammi when she comes to the phone."

Louise hesitated, trying to decide whether or not to get Tammi. She suspected that the person on the other end was Miss Mathilde because of her voice and dictatorial manner.

"Just a minute," Louise said finally. She put her hand on the receiver and motioned to Tammi. "I think it's Miss Mathilde for you," she whispered.

Tammi's eyes flashed. "I won't talk to her!" she declared.

"You'd better," Louise told her. "We'll all stand nearby and help you answer if she asks about anything you don't want her to know."

Tammi started to shake, but took Louise's advice and picked up the phone. "Hello? Who is this?"

The caller replied that she was Miss Mathilde Price. "I've been so worried about you, honey. Do tell me how you are."

"I'm fine," Tammi replied.

"Have you missed me?"

Tammi looked to the Danas for an answer. They nodded to indicate she was to say yes. Tammi did so, but said no more.

"I'm glad," Miss Mathilde said. "I hope to be back soon. Just as quickly as I can get away from my kidnappers."

Tammi burst out, "I don't want you back! I'm

staying with nice people and having a lot of fun!"

"Why, you saucy imp!" Miss Mathilde cried out angrily. "It was your grandfather's wish that I take care of you, and I intend to do so."

"Mr. Hunter doesn't agree with you."

"Is that so?" the woman exclaimed. "I took a letter to him, proving that Mr. Hodge wanted me to be your guardian!"

Before the Danas could stop Tammi, she cried, "We think the letter was forged!"

Miss Mathilde shouted into the phone that she wanted to know who "we" were. "I suppose it's those Dana girls you went to see. The so-called detectives. Well, I'm telling you right now, they're no good at all. The sooner you get away from them, the better." There was a slight pause, then the woman continued, "Tammi, you know I love you. We shouldn't fight. Tell me, what have you been doing?"

Tammi turned to her friends. Aunt Harriet and the girls each put a finger over her lips, indicating that Tammi was not to reveal anything.

"Are you still there?" Miss Mathilde asked impatiently. "Come on now, dearie, tell me what you've been doing."

Tammi replied, "Oh, just playing."

Once more the woman became angry. She cried out, "None of that! I want an answer, and a truthful one!"

Tammi looked helplessly at the Danas, who had heard men's voices in the background. Evidently they were advising Miss Mathilde what to say. Were they her "kidnappers"?

"Tammi!" the woman yelled. "Why don't you answer me?"

Tammi replied, "I've done lots of things, walked the grounds, and I've been to town shopping."

The girl paused, trying to think how to proceed and Louise whispered in her ear, "Ask her where she is."

When Miss Mathilde heard the question, she replied, "I can't say." Abruptly she hung up.

Tammi's heart was beating furiously. She flopped down on the couch and put her head against the pillow. "I can't stand that woman, and I won't let her take care of me any more!" she cried out, tears coming into her eyes.

Aunt Harriet sat beside her and took one of the girl's hands into her own. "I don't think you need to worry. Even if Miss Mathilde is not in league with her kidnappers, we'll talk to Mr. Hunter and he'll see to it that you have a better guardian."

This made Tammi feel better. She sat up and hugged Miss Dana. "You're the dearest person in the whole world!"

Aunt Harriet smiled. "What are you planning to do this afternoon?"

"I think we'll check the rest of the house for loose floorboards," Tammi replied with a grin.

Louise and Jean joined her, and the hours passed quickly, but nothing more was found. Finally a car arrived, and Homer barked happily.

"That must be Mr. Fife," Jean said and hurried to the door. The detective walked in with a friendly smile. "Hello, everybody. Any excitement here today?"

The group refrained from telling him about the safe, but said there had been no prowlers or other trouble around the grounds.

"Good. I just met the officer who is patrolling the property, and he hasn't seen anyone in the past two days."

"Have the police received any leads to Miss Mathilde's kidnappers?" Louise inquired.

"No, unfortunately, they haven't. And Ben Rush isn't talking, either."

"Maybe we finally scared our enemies off," Jean said, chuckling, then told Mr. Fife about Tammi's phone call.

The detective agreed that the conversation, with the background of men's voices, was suspicious.

"No doubt they were telling her what to say," he remarked.

"I'm convinced," Jean added, "that Mathilde Price is part of Zavier Roundtree's gang. If she had been kidnapped, her captors wouldn't allow her to make social phone calls like the one to Tammi."

Mr. Fife nodded. "I'm inclined to agree with you. Even if she should show up tomorrow, I'd be very suspicious that she was up to no good. As it is, the last thing we want is for her to come back and take care of Tammi."

"You're right!" Tammi said. "I've been so happy with the Danas and they've been so good to me that I hope things stay just the way they are now."

Mr. Fife smiled, and Louise said, "Don't worry, Tammi. Even after we have solved the mystery, we'll all be going to the same school together. You see, we'll be your friends forever!"

"That's true," Aunt Harriet said. "And now I think we should go home. I'd better call Cora before it gets too late and tell her to do some shopping for me tomorrow on her way to the house. Excuse me just a moment."

Miss Dana went to the phone and lifted the receiver. There was no sound. She jiggled the knobs on the instrument several times, but still the familiar humming sound was missing.

"Something's wrong here," Aunt Harriet called out. "The line is dead!"

Mr. Fife frowned and took the receiver from her hand. He listened, then put it down.

"This is strange," he said. "We haven't had a

storm or a notice that the phone would be turned off temporarily, have we?"

"No," Aunt Harriet said.

"And besides," Jean added, "Tammi used it just a little while ago."

"Oh, Jean," Tammi burst out, frightened, "do you think the line has been cut?"

CHAPTER XVII

Earthquake!

Mr. Fife said he once worked for the telephone company and would see if he could trace the trouble. He carefully examined the instrument itself, then the wires leading through the house. He found nothing wrong.

"I'll go outside and check," he said. "If you don't mind, I wish you would stay here and watch the house while I follow the outdoor line."

The Danas agreed, and the detective went off. He was gone about half an hour while the girls discussed what could have happened. Finally he returned.

"I located the trouble," Mr. Fife said. "The wires were cut."

Louise asked, "How long would it take for someone to come up from the road and do this?"

"Not long," Mr. Fife replied. "The line was disconnected near the main road, and if the culprit staked out the place and waited until the patrol car went by, he would have had plenty of time before the officer passed the spot again."

The detective turned to Tammi. "Where can I find a tall ladder?"

"There's one in the building that used to be a barn." She offered to go with him and show him. They soon reappeared and Mr. Fife went down the hill, carrying the ladder. It was not long before he returned and said he had spliced the wires.

"Your phone will work now, but I'll report the trouble to the company so they can make permanent repairs."

Aunt Harriet decided it was too late to catch Cora at the Dana home. "I'll call her at her own house when we get back. Let's go!"

That evening Louise and Jean had a call from the boys, who wanted to know what had happened after they left. Louise brought them up-to-date on the mystery, and ended by telling them about the cut telephone wire.

Ken exclaimed, "No doubt one of your enemies did it."

"I'm sure you're right," Louise answered. "But the question is, which one?"

After the conversation ended, the girls tried to figure out how many people were involved in the mystery.

"At this point I know of seven," Louise said. "Zavier Roundtree, Ben Rush, the man who brought the vicious dog here, the two bearded characters who tied up Tammi, and the two masked burglars who broke into our house."

"The two bearded men and the masked intruders could have been Roundtree and one of the others in disguise," Louise said. "That would bring it down to three."

"Remember that fellow we found in the house with Miss Mathilde once?" Tammi spoke up. "She said he asked her for money but she wouldn't let us call the police? He's probably in with them, too."

"Whatever their number," Jean said, "they're after big stakes. Is it the manuscript, or what may be buried in the mountain peak?"

Louise shrugged, then the girls went to bed. The following morning they were up early, eager to return to the Hodge home and investigate some more.

When they reached it, Homer greeted them enthusiastically. Mr. Fife said there had been no intruders in the house, but both he and the dog had heard three shrill whistles, one right after the other.

"I went out with a bright searchlight and beamed it all around, but could find no one," the detective added.

Jean asked, "Were the whistles close?"

"Very close. I'm sure whoever did it was on the grounds. But as I've already told you, we checked everywhere, including the outbuildings, but spotted nobody."

Mr. Fife smiled. "Just one more mystery added to this puzzling case."

Then he said good-bye and drove off, leaving Tammi and the Danas discussing the strange event.

"Maybe it wasn't as close as Mr. Fife thought," Jean suggested. "Due to the topography of the mountain, it might just have sounded that way."

Louise shrugged. "Since we can't solve that mystery, let's go to work in the basement again."

The three girls took surgical masks and went downstairs into the secret passageway. They beamed their lights into the hole they had dug and wondered what to do next.

"How would it be," Louise asked, "if we take that long ladder and climb to the lower level to investigate."

"Say, that's long," Jean said. "How will we take it down those narrow cellar steps?"

"I'll pick up the front end, you'll take the rear, and Tammi can supervise," Louise suggested. "Come on, let's try."

The girls had no problem carrying the ladder into the house. It was made of aluminium and not very heavy. But when they reached the basement door, they ran into trouble.

Louise had already descended a few steps, when Tammi cried, "Hold it! Jean's end is stuck."

"Maybe if I lower my end, and Jean raises hers,

we'll make it," Louise said and bent down as far as she could. Jean lifted the ladder high over her head, but still they could not clear the corner. Then Jean stumbled slightly and gave the ladder an involuntary push.

"Hey! You're shoving me down the stairs!" Louise protested. "Have a heart!"

Suddenly all three broke out in laughter. Come back, Louise," Tammi said. "It's just too long to work."

"I feel like a crab," Louise said with a chuckle as she moved up the stairs backwards. It seemed easier than turning around.

"Not so fast!" Jean shrieked. "My end is scratching the wall!"

Finally the girls managed to return the ladder to the outbuilding. They put it in its place, and Louise stretched her aching arms. "What'll we do now?" she wanted to know.

"Let's ask Aunt Harriet if we have a shorter one at home," Jean suggested. "If so, we can bring it over tomorrow."

They had just started to consult Miss Dana in the dining room, when the whole house started to shake violently!

Tammi shrieked in horror and looked around wildly. "What's going on?"

Before anyone could guess, several pictures fell off the walls, and furniture slid out of place.

"It's an earthquake!" Louise cried out.

"Hide!" Aunt Harriet ordered. "Get under anything heavy and unlikely to move."

The tremor seemed to subside, but Jean and Louise slipped under the dining-room table anyway. Tammi ran into the living room and chose a couch that had not been disturbed, and Aunt Harriet hurried into the hall closet.

Just then a second tremor occurred. The large dining-room chandelier crashed to the table and everyone was afraid that the whole house would come down!

"Run outside. Away from the house!" Aunt Harriet ordered. "Quick!" She led the way into the garden. The girls followed and looked around, not knowing what to do next.

Tammi was clinging to Miss Dana. "Oh, I hope there won't be a volcanic eruption like the one long ago!" she wailed in fright.

No one replied, but Louise and Jean realized that suddenly everything was quiet again. Homer, who had been barking and whining during the quake, stopped and calmed down.

Louise remembered how sensitive animals are to any kind of danger. Since the dog had ceased barking she concluded that the trouble was over.

"I guess we can go back in," she called to the others.

The girls trooped into the living room with the

idea of straightening out the furniture and putting the pictures back in place. Aunt Harriet, meanwhile, checked the kitchen.

"Oh!" she cried out. "Half the dishes are smashed!"

The girls hurried to her side to see the damage. There was a dull thud below them, which appeared to be a muffled explosion. The next moment the house shook again!

Frantic, the four rushed outdoors. By the time they reached the garden, the tremor had ceased.

"That must have been an aftermath of the earthquake," Louise deduced.

The group waited several minutes before returning inside. After surveying the damage, the Danas told Tammi they were sorry so many things had been ruined.

She answered, "That doesn't matter as long as you people are all right—and me, too!"

Aunt Harriet said she would phone the Danas' next-door neighbour to see what had happened in Oak Falls. To their amazement they learned that there had been no earthquake!

"I'll call a friend on the other side of town," Louise said and dialled the number. She, too, was told that there had been no tremor in the area.

"Let's get in touch with the nearest state-trooper headquarters," Jean said. The officer who answered thought she was joking. "There hasn't been an earthquake in this area as long as I can remember." He chuckled. "What made you think there was?"

When Jean told him, he advised her to call the local police. "Maybe someone caused an explosion at your house," he added.

Jean put the phone down. "You know, I think he's right," she told the others. "I'll bet our enemies have found a way to get underneath this place and set off a series of time bombs."

"Probably they did it last night," Louise agreed. "And the whistling Mr. Fife heard was their signal!" She called Chief Ignari, and shortly a police officer arrived. He investigated the whole house, but found nothing.

"If your suspicions are correct, I think you should leave right away," he said. "It doesn't seem safe here." Then he drove off.

Tammi looked frightened again. "Perhaps he's right," she said. "Everything has gone wrong since Grandpa's death, and if this keeps up we might all be killed!"

She started to sob. "He never harmed anyone in his whole life. I don't understand why people are doing this to me now!"

It took the Danas several minutes to calm Tammi. Then they discussed whether they should take the officer's advice.

"If we do," Louise said practically, "we're playing right into our enemies' hands. I don't believe they'll blow up the house, because they're interested in finding the duplicate manuscript or whatever they're looking for. All these schemes are just scare tactics to get us out of here!"

Aunt Harriet, who was usually cautious and against taking risks, agreed. "Why don't we put everything to rights again, and then try to figure out how these men set off the bombs? Perhaps there is a hidden entrance into the mountain!"

"That's a wonderful idea!" Jean said, and they went to work. When Tammi's home was straightened out, the three girls gathered flashlights, whistles, and shovels. They walked around the peak and completed one full turn without discovering anything.

Aunt Harriet stood near the front door and waved to them.

"No luck yet," Jean called to her, and Miss Dana suggested that they go a little farther down the slope and make another circular tour. The girls descended a hundred feet, then began walking again. Halfway around the mountain, they saw a rock formation, which caused them to pause.

"That could have been the entrance to a cave at one time," Louise remarked.

"But how would anyone get inside?" Tammi asked. "It looks solid!"

Jean went close and discovered that the bushes growing in front of the rocks were not rooted in the ground.

"Come and look!" she called to Louise and

Tammi. "These bushes are planted in big pots!"

"How amazing!" Louise exclaimed. "What wonderful camouflage."

When the three girls picked up the pots and set them aside, they realized that the bushes had indeed covered the entrance to a cave. They beamed their flashlights into the yawning hole and noticed that there was no volcanic ash on the ground.

"Are we going in?" Tammi asked. "Suppose there is another earthquake or whatever it was that shook the house?"

"Why don't you wait here?" Louise suggested. "If Jean and I have any trouble in the cave, we'll blow our whistles. Then you can dash back to the house and get help."

"I don't want to be left alone," Tammi replied. "Please let me go with you. I'm not afraid."

"Okay," Louise said. "But I think we'd better put the potted bushes back in place. If the people who camouflaged this entrance come by, they won't be suspicious."

As soon as everything was in order, the three girls went inside, beaming their lights ahead. The ceiling of the cave was about seven feet high so they did not have to stoop. The walls were rocky and looked even and undisturbed. Louise, Jean, and Tammi walked on, wondering what they would find at the end of the cave.

Finally Jean said, "I doubt that this is a cave.

It seems more like a passageway that goes deep into the mountain."

The girls stopped. All had the same thought. Were they walking into danger?

CHAPTER XVIII

Followed!

LOUISE and Jean exchanged worried glances. "What's the matter?" Tammi asked.

"We may be walking into real danger," Louise answered. "One of us should return to the entrance and wait. If the other two don't come back within a half hour, she should go for help."

Jean nodded. "It would be better than having us get into a fix."

"Okay," Tammi said. "I'll go."

"We'll come with you to make sure you'll be safe," Louise said.

As the three reached the cave entrance, Homer bounded up to them.

"Hi, old fellow," Jean said. "Did you come to act as bodyguard?"

The beautiful dog stopped in front of her. As she looked at him, Jean realized that a folded note was tied to his collar. Quickly she took it off and opened the sheet. "It's from Aunt Harriet," she exclaimed.

"What does it say?" Louise asked.

Jean read, "Thought you might need the dog. A stranger called. He said if the Dana girls don't leave the property at once, they'll be in serious trouble."

A look of fright came over Tammi's face. "Another threat!" she said. "I just can't put you in such danger. Maybe we should give up. Why don't we go to your house?"

Louise hugged the intimidated girl and said that she and Jean never backed out when they were solving a mystery.

"We're going to see this through, and nobody's going to stop us!"

Tammi looked at her with admiration. "You're so wonderful. My grandpa knew what he was doing when he told me to find you and ask for your help."

Louise had a suggestion. "How about my staying outside with Homer and standing guard? You two go into the passageway and see where it leads."

She and the dog positioned themselves behind the bushes, where they could not be seen, while Jean and Tammi hurried into the tunnel.

"You know what I think?" Jean said, beaming

her light around. "This must have been dug after the last eruption of the volcano."

"You mean because it's so perfect and there's no trace of ash?" Tammi asked.

"Yes," Jean replied.

Both girls scanned every inch of the walls, ceiling, and floor, but saw nothing unusual.

"This has to go somewhere," Tammi remarked.

"You're right," Jean agreed. "It may even lead to your house," she added as the tunnel began sloping upward.

The girls walked in silence for several minutes. Suddenly they were confronted with a solid dirt wall! They stopped and stared at it.

"I guess it's the end," Tammi said. "The tunnel didn't lead anywhere after all. Too bad we didn't find any clues."

Jean touched the wall and scooped up a handful of dirt. "That hasn't been here long," she said thoughtfully. "It's too soft. The walls and ceiling and floor are rocky, and somehow this blockade doesn't seem natural."

"What are you getting at?" Tammi asked.

"I'm not sure, but this may have been the place where the explosives were set. They made all this dirt rain down and created an artificial wall. Maybe it's not very wide. Let's dig and see if we can make a hole in it."

The two girls unstrapped the shovels they were

carrying on their backs and began to work vigorously. It was not long before they had made an opening large enough to crawl through.

"Shall we continue our search?" Tammi wanted to know.

"Yes," Jean replied. "I have an idea we'll find something important."

Just as they were about to climb through the hole, a light came up behind them. A moment later a voice called out, "Jean, Tammi, are you there?"

Louise! She hurried up to them with Homer at her side.

"What's the matter?" Jean asked apprehensively.

Her sister was out of breath and obviously agitated. "Someone's coming!" she said in a hoarse whisper. "Homer suddenly raised his ears to listen. I told him not to bark, because I didn't want him to give away our position."

"Then what happened?" Jean urged.

"I spotted two men in the distance. They were walking up the hillside in the direction of the cave!"

Tammi and Jean stared at Louise as they realized the implications of her observation.

"If they come in here, we're trapped!" Jean exclaimed.

"I know," Louise said. "But there was no place for me to hide. Anyway, I thought I should warn you, and let Homer scare away any visitors." Then she added hopefully, "Maybe the men won't notice the entrance!"

"I don't think we should count on that," Jean said. "We'd better look for cover."

"Let's crawl through the hole and hide," Tammi suggested.

"Good idea," Jean said. "And whisper so the men won't hear us if they come in."

Quickly the girls picked up their shovels and wriggled through the hole. Homer followed, and Louise beamed her light ahead. The tunnel continued, but there was no visible crevice or outcropping where they could hide.

"Shall we go on?" Jean asked.

Just then the girls heard men's voices.

"They're here!" Louise whispered. "We mustn't let them see our lights and we can't go on in the dark. Let's stay right here. Put out your flashes and don't move!"

Jean, Louise, Tammi, and Homer huddled together to one side. Tammi started to shake with fear. She remembered that one of their enemies had brought a gun to the Hodge property recently. If he had it with him now, he could use it on them and no one would ever find them!

Jean put an arm around the younger girl. "Don't panic," she whispered. "It's important to keep your wits in a situation like this."

The girls sat in silence as the voices became

more distinct. Homer bristled, but Louise laid her hand on his back, telling him to sit still.

Two men were approaching, and one said with a chuckle, "I guess our explosion brought down a lot of dirt."

His companion beamed a light straight ahead. "Zavier, look at the hole!"

Zavier Roundtree!

"I don't think the explosion could have done that!" Zavier declared.

"You're right! Somebody's been in here digging!"

"Yeah," Zavier replied. "Matter of fact, Menzie, someone could be in this tunnel right now!"

He sounded worried, and both men stood still for a moment. Then they moved forward, and Zavier shone his flashlight through the opening.

Homer could not keep still any longer. He jumped up, put his front paws on the edge of the hole, and growled menacingly.

"The dog!" Menzie cried out. "He'll chew us to pieces! Let's get out of here!"

The men turned and ran down the passageway as quickly as they could. Obviously they carried no weapons and were at the mercy of the menacing police dog!

Jean, Louise, and Tammi breathed sighs of relief. "Thank goodness they're gone!" Tammi exclaimed as the girls turned on their flashlights.

"Yes," said Jean. "And do you realize we picked

up a good clue? One of Zavier's pals is named Menzie!"

"That's right," Louise replied. She leaned over and patted Homer. "Good dog," she said. "You probably saved our lives!"

"I'm sure the men think Homer wriggled past the artificial entrance," Jean said. "And they figure he dug the hole while investigating!" She hugged the German shepherd gratefully.

Homer wagged his tail in delight, and looked up at the girl, then whined as he begged to be told what to do next.

Tammi got up and stretched her cramped muscles. "Are we going back?" she wanted to know.

"I don't think we should quit," Louise said, beaming her flashlight on the section that had not yet been investigated. "I'm sure the men won't return for some time. Homer frightened them, and that gives us a chance to check out this passageway farther."

Jean agreed. "We're probably safer now than we'll ever be. Are you game, Tammi?"

"Sure," she said bravely, though the Danas felt she would have preferred to leave.

"Okay," Jean said. "Suppose Tammi and I go ahead. Louise, do you mind staying here and keeping watch with Homer just in case we run into trouble? If we're not back in fifteen minutes, get Aunt Harriet."

"Will do," Louise said and settled herself beside the hole while Tammi and Jean started off.

Again the tunnel turned upward. They were climbing the mountain.

Tammi took Jean's hand. "Where do you think this passageway will end?" she asked.

CHAPTER XIX

Sealed Exit!

As LOUISE waited with the dog near the dirt wall, she kept thinking about the two men who had shown up in the passageway. They were Zavier Roundtree and a pal named Menzie. But who was he? His voice had seemed vaguely familiar, and Louise tried hard to remember where she had heard it before.

Suddenly the answer came to her. He was the man who had allegedly held up Miss Mathilde for money when the Danas had first visited the Hodge house with Tammi!

"There's no doubt now that Mathilde Price is in league with the gang," Louise decided. "That's why she didn't want the police called. This man wasn't asking her for money—he was arguing about something else!"

Louise was so deep in thought that she hardly

noticed Homer. He had begun to whine and finally put both paws on the girl's shoulders.

Louise snapped out of her pensive mood and said, "What is it, Homer?"

The dog jumped up to the edge of the hole and started to go through it. Louise pulled him back. "We have to stay here until Jean and Tammi return," she told him.

Meanwhile, the two girls were walking on and on, beaming their lights around. As they proceeded, ash began to appear on the floor and became deeper and deeper as they went along.

"This is odd," Jean remarked. "The first part of the tunnel had no ash; now there's a lot of it."

"You're right," Tammi said. "That ancient volcano powdered this place."

"But why only half?"

"I have an idea," Tammi said. "Suppose *this* part of the tunnel is prehistoric. At one time it could have been a connection to the passageway running under the house. Grandpa might have discovered it and found that it didn't go all the way out to the side of the mountain. So he extended it and that's why the other part of the tunnel has no ash."

The girls went around another bend, then stopped short. A blank stone wall faced them!

"The end!" Tammi exclaimed in disappointment. "It doesn't lead anywhere."

Jean examined the wall carefully. Then she declared. "I believe this is the foundation of your house. See how smoothly those stones have been put together, not like jagged rocks in the tunnel?"

"You mean," Tammi asked, "that at one time there was a hole in the foundation and anyone in the house could walk right through here?"

"Yes. There's a light line of cement running up, across, and down this section of the wall. I'm sure there was once an opening here, but someone closed it."

"Let's find out as fast as we can," Tammi urged and banged her shovel against the stones. It made no impression.

Both girls realized it was impossible to proceed without chisels and hammers.

Tammi offered to go to the house for them. "I'm familiar with the mountain, and can take a shortcut."

"Okay," Jean agreed. "Tell Louise what we've found and you'd better take the dog with you."

"I'll hurry," Tammi promised and started off on a run. Jean called after her, "Ask Louise to come here!"

Minutes later Louise appeared. She was astounded at the discovery, and began to dig in the ash floor.

"This may be the hiding place for the artifacts that are missing from Grandpa Hodge's list," she said.

"Could be," Jean agreed, and put her shovel into the gray-white dust.

They worked silently for a while. Louise hit something hard. She reached down and picked up a small statuette.

"An artifact!" the girl detective exclaimed, brushing off the dust.

"What is it?" Jean asked.

"This looks like a doll. Maybe some prehistoric child once played with it."

The Danas were so excited by the find that they paid little attention to their watering eyes until Louise began to sneeze.

"Do you have a handkerchief?" Jean asked her and pulled one out of her own pocket.

Louise nodded and both girls covered their noses and mouths with the kerchiefs and tied them at the back of their heads. Then they continued looking for artifacts. Presently Jean discovered several cutting and polishing tools.

"Do you suppose they belonged to ancient jewellers?" she asked.

Before Louise could answer, Tammi appeared, loaded down with tools and surgical masks. From a leather thong around her neck hung chisels and hammers, and she was carrying a pickaxe.

"I ran as fast as I could," she said, trying to breath deeply to offset her panting.

"Where's Homer?" Louise asked.

"I left him with Aunt Harriet. She was worried

and said she had a hunch there might be trouble at the house because of that threatening phone call. Anyway, she notified the police and they promised to send over a couple of men."

"Maybe we should all go back and stay with Aunt Harriet until they arrive," Louise said.

"No, your aunt said she would come to look for us with the officers as soon as they got there."

The Danas decided to go on with their work. They showed Tammi the artifacts they had found and put them into their pockets. Then, using the new tools, the three hacked at the cement outline in the wall. After a while stones tumbled out. When there was a large enough hole for the girls to look through, Louise beamed her light into it, but it was not strong enough to penetrate the darkness.

"Can you see anything?" Tammi asked.

Louise shook her head, so all three girls shone their flashlights inside to get a clearer view.

Louise cried out, "This place has a solid wall at the back, and I see something standing there that appears to be a machine."

She shouted through the opening, "Can anyone hear me?" The only answer was a hollow echo.

At that moment Jean turned her flashlight downwards. "Look!" she cried out. "There are lots of papers on the floor!"

The three girls stared at them. Louise said, "We'll climb through and see what they are."

Tammi became excited. "Maybe it's Grandpa's duplicate manuscript!"

She and the Danas wriggled through the hole. As Tammi eagerly collected the pages, Louise and Jean examined the small room.

"I don't believe it!" Jean exclaimed, shining her flashlight on the piece of old machinery. "This looks like an ancient generator of some kind."

"Jean! Do you suppose this room was part of Grandpa Hodge's lab at one time?" Louise asked.

"I wouldn't be surprised," her sister replied. "What's all that stuff over in the right-hand corner?"

Both girls investigated and their mouths dropped open. "Artifacts!" Jean burst out. "All of them polished and shiny and stacked up neatly in a pile!"

"How many are there?" Louise asked.

As Jean picked up each one, she counted. Finally she declared, "Twenty-four! They must be the ones Grandpa Hodge described on the list we found in the safe!"

"Forget about the artifacts for a while and help me with these pages," Tammi said, and the girls joined her. They shone their lights on the papers and quickly read some of the sheets.

"This *is* the manuscript!" Tammi cried out in delight. "There's the title page. It says *The Pumas' Treasure*."

"I can't wait to read the whole thing," Jean said. "But it'll take us a while to put the entire manuscript in order. I wonder why Grandpa Hodge scattered it around like this."

"He may not have," Louise suggested. "The explosions could have done this."

"You're right," Jean agreed. "Wait, here's a letter to Littleton Books, a publisher."

As she read, the other two girls looked over her shoulder. In the letter Mr. Hodge explained that his research had shown that the mountain at one time had been an active volcano, and that a tribe of people who lived in the area worshipped the puma as their god. He had found various artifacts, and the book was a fictional account based on what he had discovered.

Grandpa Hodge realized that the objects were very valuable and had arranged to sell them to a museum when the book came out.

"This is fantastic!" Jean exclaimed. "I wonder—"

She stopped short as the place suddenly began to shake. Small stones separated from the ceiling and hailed onto the girls. Dust rose from the floor, and Jean started to cough despite her kerchief mask.

All three sat down until the tremor ceased. They stared at one another in puzzlement and fright.

"No doubt our enemies set off another bomb!" Louise said tensely.

There was stunned silence for a few seconds as the girls realized the implications of Louise's statement.

"We'd better get out of here as fast as we can," Jean said finally.

Leaving the artifacts and their tools behind, but taking the manuscript with them, the three ran across the ash floor.

"Hurry!" Louise called. She was in the lead with Jean behind her and Tammi bringing up the rear.

Suddenly Tammi cried out in pain. The Danas turned. "What's the matter?" Louise asked her.

"My ankle! I slipped and hurt it," Tammi said, on the verge of tears.

Jean put an arm around her. "Sit down and I'll examine your ankle."

Jean took off Tammi's shoe and felt all around the girl's foot. "Where does it hurt?" she asked.

"Right there," Tammi said. "You just had your finger on it."

Jean gently massaged the spot. "Does it feel better?"

"I—I think so." Tammi put her shoe back on and got to her feet. "It still hurts with my weight on it, but I can walk."

"Lean on me as much as you can," Jean advised and took Tammi's arm.

"Okay."

The three girls went on, and soon reached the

wall barrier. The tremor had loosened more dirt and stones from the ceiling and sides, and the opening had disappeared! The wall was as solid as it had been before!"

Their exit was sealed off! The girls were trapped!

CHAPTER XX

Surprise Confession

In the Hodge house Aunt Harriet was frantic. The tremor had shaken the building, though less violently than the previous explosions, which she and the girls had mistaken for an earthquake.

Homer was running around in a frenzy, scratching on the front door and trying to get out. Suddenly he barked loudly.

At the same time Miss Dana heard a car drive up. She hurried to a window. To her relief she saw Ken, Chris, and Paul get out and walk toward the door.

She hastened to let them in. "I'm so glad you're here!" she exclaimed.

"Are you all right?" Chris asked. "The earth seemed to shake as we reached the top of the hill."

"The crooks must have set off another explosion," Aunt Harriet said. "I'm worried sick about the girls!"

"Where are they?"

"In the tunnel where the first detonation took place," Miss Dana said and explained about her nieces' investigation.

Paul looked shocked. "Is Tammi with them?"

"She carried tools to Jean and Louise."

Ken asked, "Where is the passageway? We must rescue the girls at once!"

"I don't know, but Homer does. He can lead you to it," Miss Dana replied.

"Good. We'll need a flashlight and shovels in case we have to dig."

"I'll get them right away." Aunt Harriet brought a light, two shovels, a pick, a leash for the dog, and surgical masks, and handed them to the boys. "I'll stay here because I called the police. They should arrive any minute."

"Let's go!" Chris urged. He fastened the leash to Homer, who ran so fast that it was hard for the boys to keep up with him.

Soon they reached the cave entrance. The farther they got into the tunnel, the dustier it became. Debris and loose stones shaken from the walls made walking difficult.

Chris said tensely, "I hope the girls aren't buried under a heap of rubble!"

The three pushed forward and finally came to

the wall barrier. Homer barked, and the boys shouted.

Did they hear a muffled reply? Without hesitation, they began to dig. It seemed like hours before they heard a scraping noise from the other side.

Ken wiped beads of perspiration from his forehead. "Anybody there?" he called out.

"Yes, we're here," was the faint answer. "Thank goodness you found us! Keep digging!"

The boys worked with renewed vigour. Suddenly there was a sound of metal clanging against metal, and the next moment they broke through the wall. Chris had banged Jean's shovel. The girls had been working on the barrier from the other side!

"Hey, you don't have to hit me!" Jean called out in an attempt to break the tension. "All we want you to do is to rescue us!"

"Give us two more minutes and we'll oblige," Ken promised and the boys made the hole large enough for one person to wriggle through.

"Wait until we're sure there won't be a cave-in," said Chris.

He inched his way to the other side, and Homer followed. The dog yapped happily and jumped up on the girls, while Chris hugged them, a big smile of relief on his face.

"We sure are glad to see you!" he said. "We were scared silly you might have been buried!"

"We could have been," Jean said. "Luckily we were too far away. But we might have suffocated before we could have dug our way out!"

"What exactly happened?" Chris asked.

Louise explained. "We discovered a secret room a short distance from here. When the place started to shake, we left our tools behind and ran. But when we reached this wall, our escape was blocked."

"This barrier wasn't here when you went in?"

"Yes, but it was smaller. We made an opening through it and went deeper into the tunnel. When we came back, the hole was filled up and the debris much thicker. We rushed back for our shovels, but we would have smothered before we could have dug our way out!"

"Not only that," Tammi added, "we were afraid those horrible men might have left another bomb with a timer that could explode any minute and bury us!"

"We'd better hurry and get out of here right away," Chris said.

Ken and Paul, who had stuck their heads through the hole, withdrew and helped the girls crawl to the other side with the tools they had brought.

As Tammi wriggled out, the statuette Louise had discovered fell from her pocket.

"What's this?" Chris asked and picked it up.

"We think it's a doll," Jean replied. "We found it—and we also found the duplicate manuscript!"

Ken, Chris, and Paul looked admiringly at the girls.

"You're wonderful!" Ken exclaimed. "Best sleuths in the world." He stuffed the statuette into his pocket and grinned. "This is the first time I ever carried a doll!"

Paul picked up a shovel. "Come on, take the tools and let's get out of here."

The six young people hurried on with Homer in the lead. When they reached the cave entrance, a surprise awaited them. Not only was Aunt Harriet there, but also Mr. Fife and Officers Rad and Buxton.

"We were just about to come in," Mr. Fife said as Homer greeted him joyously. "Are you all right?"

"We're dirty and have a few bruises," Jean replied, "but otherwise we're fine."

"Thank goodness!" Aunt Harriet said and hugged the girls, trying to hold back tears of relief.

"Guess what we found!" Tammi exclaimed triumphantly. "The duplicate manuscript!"

She told the onlookers about their discovery and explained its significance.

"That certainly is a great find," Mr. Fife said. "We've something to tell you, too. When your aunt phoned the police and reported the threatening call, I had a hunch that today was the day things would happen on the mountain peak."

"You were right," Jean said.

"And how!" Mr. Fife went on. "My colleagues and I arrived just in time to see two men racing down the hill. We caught them!"

"Zavier Roundtree and Menzie," Jean said.

"Yes. But how did you know?"

"We overheard them talking in the passageway," the girl replied. "They called each other by name."

"Why don't we go back to the house and I'll tell you the whole story," Mr. Fife suggested. "Roundtree and his pal Menzie Rice have confessed everything."

"Wonderful," Louise said. "But before we wash and change clothes, we'd like to check the walls in Grandpa Hodge's lab."

As soon as the group arrived at the mountain-peak home, the young people disappeared into the cellar. They went into the laboratory and turned on the lights.

"I'm sure the secret room was once part of this place," Louise said. "Grandpa Hodge must have had access to it from here so he could hide the manuscript and the artifacts."

"But why did he put some in the safe?" Tammi asked.

"Perhaps he had been cataloguing them and

hadn't had a chance to bring them down here," Jean replied. "Come on, let's examine the walls thoroughly."

The girls checked every square foot of the fieldstone as far as they could reach, while the boys examined the top part.

Suddenly Jean cried out, "Look, some of these stones are loose! They come right out!"

The others ran over to her and together they removed a number of perfectly fitted rocks at the bottom of the back wall. Soon they created an opening three feet wide and four feet high. As they had suspected, the secret room was on the other side!

Tammi was so excited she could hardly stand still. "Wait until we tell the others!" she exclaimed. "Come on, let's hurry back upstairs!"

"Why don't we take the artifacts?" Chris asked. "If everyone carries a few, we'll be able to bring them all up."

"Good idea," Jean said, and each took some of the relics.

When they reached the living room and displayed the artifacts, the others gasped in amazement.

"Fantastic!" Mr. Fife exclaimed. "You finally found Grandpa Hodge's treasure!"

Officer Rad chuckled. "Girls, if you ever want a job with the police force, let me know. We can use some class-A detectives!"

Mr. Fife smiled. "Now let me tell you what I learned from Roundtree. He's Mathilde Price's cousin. Mathilde, as you know, had been a friend of Grandpa Hodge's and had visited him occasionally."

"I never met her before he died," Tammi said.

Mr. Fife nodded. "She usually dropped by when you were in school. Once, while your grandfather left his den, she noticed the manuscript he was working on. She quickly read parts of it and told her cousin."

"So that's how Roundtree found out about it!" Tammi exclaimed. "And to think Grandpa trusted that woman!"

"Unfortunately, he did. Roundtree smelled money and persuaded Mathilde to steal the work. They took it to their close friend, Ben Rush, who had studied archeology and was knowledgeable about ancient artifacts.

"Roundtree and Rush examined the manuscript, but before they could finish it, a fire broke out in Rush's apartment and the valuable document burned."

"That's why they wanted the copy!" Jean said.

"Of course. They realized that there must be a duplicate at Hodge's home, and were trying to figure out a way to get it, when Grandpa Hodge died. At that point, Rush had the idea of planting Mathilde Price as Tammi's guardian by presenting a phony letter to Mr. Hunter."

"And by pretending to rearrange everything in the house, she was supposed to look for the manuscript," Louise put in.

"That's correct," Mr. Fife said. "Only she didn't find it. Mathilde and her cousin realized that they literally had to take the house apart if they wanted to succeed. For that reason they needed to get Tammi out of the way."

"Were they aware that Tammi had come to us for help?" Louise asked.

"No, they weren't. But when she showed up at the house with you, they realized they'd better act fast. Roundtree worked out the fake kidnap plan. They came to the mountain peak and tied Tammi up. Then they took Mathilde out to the car, but before they could come back for Tammi, they were scared away by the Danas, who were driving up. So they rushed off in the opposite direction."

"It was a good thing we arrived at just the right moment," Jean remarked.

Tammi said with a shudder, "No telling what might have happened to me if you hadn't come."

"Their plan was to keep you confined until they found what they were looking for," Mr. Fife continued. "Then they would have released both you and Miss Mathilde and no one would have guessed that she was part of the scheme."

"What a terrible woman!" Tammi said. "She's not coming back to take care of me, is she?"

"Of course not," Mr. Fife replied. "She'll get a prison term for helping in the scheme to rob you of your rightful inheritance. Mr. Hunter was supposed to come over and tell you about your future, Tammi. He should be here soon."

"I have a question," Jean said. "Who were the bearded men that tied Tammi up?"

"Roundtree and Rush in disguise."

"And who was the man with the dog that attacked Homer?"

"Menzie's brother Arthur Rice. He returned later with a gun to scare you people out of the house. By the way, two officers are on their way to arrest him."

"And who made the threatening phone call earlier today?" Tammi asked.

"That was Roundtree. He wanted to frighten you so you'd stay in the house while he and Menzie planted the bomb. They were responsible for that first phony earthquake, too."

"They must have returned to the tunnel while Tammi and Homer went for the tools and Louise and I were digging for artifacts in front of the secret room," Jean said. "And we thought we were safe!"

"What about the package with the acid that Roundtree dropped near the entrance lane?" Louise asked. "What did he plan to do with that?"

"He hoped you'd find it and get burned," Mr. Fife answered. "Just another of his sadistic ideas.

He's really bad. By the way, it's a good thing you kept that innocent woman and her children from opening the package."

"One more thing puzzles me," Jean said. "We never learned the meaning of the triangle that Grandpa Hodge carved into the tree."

"Maybe it was just a hobby of his," Louise said. "Remember Mary Lyon telling us about his doodling and drawing lines between the stars on maps of the heavens?"

"I guess we'll never know for sure," Tammi said. "But it doesn't matter now—"

She was interrupted by the doorbell. Aunt Harriet admitted Mr. Hunter, who was quickly briefed on the day's events. He was delighted to hear that the mystery had been solved.

Then he turned to Tammi. "I have a surprise for you," he said. "It seems best to me and the men in the trust department that you no longer live here. I've made arrangements for you to stay with Mrs. Mary Lyon, whom you like so much, and whom your grandfather found so reliable."

Tammi jumped up and clapped her hands. "I'm so happy!" she said. "Next to the Danas, I like Mrs. Lyon best of everyone I know!"

Louise and Jean were glad that Tammi was happy at last. Realizing that the case had come to an end, they suddenly longed for a new mystery to turn up. It eventually did, and involved *The Witch's Omen.*

Aunt Harriet spoke up. "Will this house be sold?" she asked Mr. Hunter.

"We have no plans to sell at this time," the banker replied. "Tammi might even want to make it an archeological museum later on and open the sccrct passageways to the public. Meanwhile, perhaps some more artifacts of the Puma people will be found, and I hereby give Louise and Jean Dana the job of locating them."

As the girls grinned, he added, "I promise there won't be any more earthquakes!"